THE JEWISH HOLIDAY HANDBOOK

DORON KORNBLUTH

Mosaica Press, Inc.

© 2014 by Mosaica Press

Typeset and designed by Rayzel Broyde

ISBN 13: 978-1-937887-29-2   ISBN-10: 937887294

MOSAICA PRESS

Published and distributed by:
Mosaica Press, Inc.
www.mosaicapress.com
info@mosaicapress.com

With thanks to the following families whose multi-faceted support helped make this project come to fruition:

The Eisenstadt Family
The Hines and Steinberg Families
The Horowitz Family
The Tabachnik Family
Other anonymous sponsors

May you enjoy much naches from your children!

Table of Contents

Acknowledgments

I began writing this book years ago. It has passed through numerous changes, revisions, and improvements. Since I started it, I have moved cities, changed jobs, and watched my family grow. All along, I've wanted to finish "the holiday book," as I have usually called it. In part, I wanted to finish what I started. Also, several friends who reviewed the book in its formative stages have repeatedly asked me about it. I would sometimes despair at the many changes required, the huge amount of material that needed to be sifted through and reduced (the book was originally 200 pages long!), and the hundreds of hours necessary for rewriting. Furthermore, I've sometimes felt that if I would start again now, the book would be very different. After all, I'm different.

In truth, I felt — and feel — that this short volume is much needed, as is. I hope you will agree.

Many friends, acquaintances, and colleagues have looked through the work at various stages of its development. These include but are not limited to: Mrs. Rivka E. Bennett, Rabbi Jonathan and Mrs. Dinah Bressel, Rabbi Jon and Mrs. Jessica Erlbaum, Mr. and Mrs. Ian Freedman, Mrs. Miriam Friedman, Mrs. Frayde Friedman, Mr. and Mrs. Daniel Green, Mrs. Suri Levine, Rabbi Tzvi and Mrs. Baila Miro, Mrs. Abra Siegel-Hiller, Rabbi Brad and Mrs. Simi Yellin. Sadly, over the many years of developing this work, including moving homes, watching helplessly as computers crash and files mistakenly get thrown out, this list is incomplete. To all those who offered time, interest, opinions, and ideas, my apologies for not keeping better track of your identities. Your contributions did not go to waste — they are incorporated within the book. Extra thanks to my dear friend and colleague, Jon Erlbaum, listed above, who never ceased reminding me about the quality and importance of this material. Thanks.

My in-laws, Jack and Joy Siegel, have been very encouraging in the development of this and my other books. Their comments on the text have been extremely useful, and have improved the work in your hands considerably. Their advice and help in all areas of our lives is most appreciated.

My parents, Harvey and Judy Kornbluth, deserve special mention. Their encouragement and support of my teaching and writing has been consistent and strong. They sacrificed much in order to provide their children with good schools, good camps, and a wholesome environment. Only now, as a parent, can I truly recognize the value of their efforts.

Finally, I turn to my wife of seventeen years, Sarah Tikvah. What can I add that I haven't already said and written? Little. But you know and I know how little I'd get done — and how miserable I'd be — without you. Thank you.

Doron Kornbluth
5774 / 2014
Israel

Foreword

By Rabbi Yaacov Haber
Rav, Kehillat Shivtei Yeshurun
Ramat Beit Shemesh, Israel

What is a Jewish Holiday?

On the simplest level, holidays are a time of celebration. In most cases, we are happy as we celebrate a historical event. At some turning point in history, Israel and the Jewish People were in trouble and G-d miraculously saved us. Every year, when that time of year comes around — again we celebrate.

On some dates, however, we celebrate tragedy. We remember, reflect and commemorate sad times, times of destruction and times of pain. It is through all of these celebrations that history is kept alive and our future becomes more secure. In all instances, it is a particular event in history that causes the date to be a holiday.

On a more profound level, it seems that the opposite is true. Time, we are taught, is a creation of G-d, just like trees, animals and humans. This creation called time can be viewed as a capsule of energy. There are time capsules of freedom, time capsules of love, time capsules of wisdom, and so unfortunately, time capsules of sadness and destruction. The Jewish calendar is a compilation of these 'energy capsules' and our holidays are merely examples of those energies playing out.

In other words, the days on the calendar have their own effect, an effect which very often repeats itself time and again throughout history. The day on the calendar is a participating cause of the events of the day. History repeats itself. Indeed, it causes itself to be repeated.

On the Ninth day of the month of *Av*, we worry about tragedy. So many tragedies have occurred on that day: the destruction of the First Temple by the Babylonians; the destruction of the Second Temple by Romans, under Titus, in the year 70 CE; the subsequent crush of the Bar Kochba revolt in the year 132; the First Crusade declared by Pope Urban II in 1095; the Inquisition in Spain and Portugal in 1492; the beginning of the First World War on the Ninth of Av 1914 — to name just a few.

During biblical times, in the month of *Nissan*, we were emancipated from slavery in Egypt. The Talmud teaches that the future messianic redemption will also take place in the month of *Nissan*.

Haman, the evil minister of Persia, searched the Jewish calendar to find the best time to annihilate the Jewish People. He chose *Adar*, as that was the month that Moses died. Little did he realize that Moses was also born in the month of *Adar* — and so, on Purim we were saved.

Rabbi Eliyahu Dessler describes the Jewish calendar as a circle, and explains that every year we travel through that same circle. It is, in fact, that very same time capsule that we encounter year after year, often with similar results.

According to this new understanding, we do not only celebrate history on the prescribed calendar date but rather we become part of the energy and history of that day. Dates, taught Rabbi Dessler, are the language of time.

Holidays are indeed Holy Days. They are separated from the rest of the year and have an energy of their own. It is from this energy that we derive the laws and appropriate practices of the holiday we encounter.

Celebrating Jewish Holidays keeps us aware of the deeper dimensions of life, allowing us to join the past with the future, as we celebrate in the present.

Rabbi Doron Kornbluth has done a great service by bringing these ancient practices to the lives of the modern reader.

May we all experience the joy of the future as we celebrate the markers of the past.

Adar 5774

Introduction

The *Shofar*. Matzah. Lighting candles. Growing up Jewish is, for many of us, really growing up with the Jewish holidays. Along with a few life cycle events, the holidays are the main Jewish landmarks we pass along the journey of life. They teach us. They inspire us. They comfort us. They remind us that we are Jewish.

Some of the holidays are widely practiced.

Others are often ignored.

Yet whether popular or not, the Jewish holidays are largely misunderstood. Of course, Chanukah *is* about light and Passover *is* about freedom, but there is so much more. Each holiday offers tremendous insights and inspiration for everyone, regardless of religious background.

For example:

Rosh Hashanah is the Jewish New Year, and thus represents a new start. A new recognition of G-d and of the Divine soul inside of us, which longs for meaning, spirituality, and community.

Yom Kippur, often experienced as sad and tortuous, is actually a happy day. G-d, Who is Perfect in all ways, knew that we weren't and therefore gave us a beautiful day to apologize, forgive, and be forgiven.

Sukkot is the time of joy. A weeklong celebration. Jewish pride. Connection. Music. Food. Friendship and family. By leaving our homes temporarily to dwell in the *Sukkah*, we appreciate our homes all the more. By waving the Four Species, we remind ourselves that meaning can be found everywhere — and that we must *act* in order to connect.

Chanukah. In the middle of winter, when all is cold and dark, G-d reminds us that He is still there. Accessible. Active. And that life is indeed ... miraculous. Lighting the candles has become one of the quintessential ways modern Jews express their Judaism. Despite the darkness, the candles remain lit. Despite the challenges, we remain Jewish.

Purim. Children dress up, *give* presents (and receive some as well!), and enjoy. Adults do the same, and yet there is so much more. G-d is never mentioned in the Scroll of Esther, unique among all the books of the Hebrew Bible, because His hand, and our destiny, is hidden. Unclear. And yet Purim reminds us to rejoice and remember — things can and do change, sometimes quickly.

Passover. On Passover, the Jewish nation was born. No one had ever left the slavery of Egypt until the ancient Hebrews did so, en masse. Through miracles, great and small, G-d was openly active in history and threw His lot in with ours. On Passover, we celebrate freedom. Jewishness. And G-d.

Shavuot. Physical freedom is wonderful. It allows people to live. Yet we were not freed simply to become like everyone else. Assimilation would have accomplished that, eventually. We were freed to be a unique People. A Light unto the Nations. A Nation of Priests. A People of the Book. On Shavuot, we received that book.

These are only a few highlights of the most famous holidays. In reality, each and every holiday has much to teach us. Still, the Jewish holidays are more than a collection of individual inspirational days. The whole is much greater than the parts. The holidays accompany us through the seasons, years, and our lives. In beautiful interdependence, they affect and reflect the entirety of our beings. They form a beautiful and intricate system. They build on each other. Yom Kippur is deep and powerful on its own, but can only be truly appreciated when it follows Rosh Hashanah. Passover is meant to set the stage for Shavuot. All the holidays work together.

That is not to say that we all must do everything tomorrow. While it may surprise you, Judaism is not all-or-nothing. For someone to begin his or her Jewish explorations with only some of the holidays, or with only some of the practices of a given holiday, is most understandable and often wise. Each step we take to connect to our Jewish identity is beautiful and inspirational. Every act counts.

Judaism is rich in holidays. In the autumn, with the High Holidays and Sukkot coming quickly one after another, they can sometimes seem overwhelming. Indeed, one of the sad facts of the modern Jewish reality is that Judaism itself can seem overwhelming. So many holidays. So many books. So much Hebrew. So much to know. No wonder so many Jews seem uninterested. Who has the time? Who has the energy?

If the holidays are experienced as a burden, it is difficult to motivate people to get involved. We already have enough burdens in our lives. Who needs more to do? Who wants extra responsibilities?

An old Jewish story tells of two merchants who arrive at an inn late at night with similar suitcases. One's bag is full of his merchandise: diamonds and precious stones. The other's bag is full of his merchandise: heavy tools. The porter joins the first merchant on the way to his room and carries his bag for him. Upon arrival at the door, the porter remarks: "You carry that every day? One of the heaviest bags I've ever carried!" The merchant responds, "If the bag you've been carrying is a heavy load, it isn't mine!" and then returns to get his own.

Judaism is not a burden. Practiced correctly, the holidays are neither "heavy" nor "boring." If you grew up with endless Passover Seders and other similar negative Jewish holiday experiences, then you have not experienced the holidays as they were meant to be experienced. G-d did not command us to suffer through negative religious experiences! Quite the opposite: the only way to properly live Jewish life is to do it with *simchah*, joy.

Judaism detests rote actions devoid of understanding or meaning. Our consciences hate this as well. So what does one do if it all seems quite "uninteresting"?

One solution is simply to stop performing empty actions. While the person won't have many traditions left, at least they'll be intellectually consistent.

A better solution, from a Jewish point of view, is to spend a little time — even a few minutes makes a world of difference — to understand the ideas and themes behind the Jewish acts we do. Thankfully, in our age, great Jewish information and education is easily available. There are dozens of books about the Jewish holidays. There are many excellent Jewish websites with sections devoted to them.

There is, in fact, so much wisdom and inspiration available about each holiday that, as we said, it can all seem quite intimidating.

And therefore, this handbook. With a short chapter on each major holiday, readers can quickly get an idea of each holiday's main activities and themes. Each chapter includes a brief description of the holiday, a summary of preparations and practices, and a short look at some of the most important relevant ideas. At the end of each chapter is a Fast Facts section to summarize the "least you need to know" in only a minute or two.

Each holiday is an amazing opportunity to take steps towards happier and more meaningful lives. Each has a world of wisdom within it. Each is a gateway into a moment, a day, or a lifetime of connection, meaning, and joy.

All we have to do is to let ourselves be inspired.

PLEASE NOTE

Buyer Beware: This handbook is a *descriptive introduction* to the major Jewish holidays. It is neither comprehensive nor a practical how-to guide of what should be done, when, and how. For information on *how* to observe the various holidays, please see the recommended reading list found at the end of the book.

Chapter 1:
Rosh Hashanah

> *On Rosh Hashanah it is written, on Yom Kippur it is sealed:*
> *How many shall pass on, how many shall come to be;*
> *Who shall live and who shall die ...*
> *But repentance, prayer, and charity can save us from the severe decree!*
>
> (Rosh Hashanah Prayers)

The Jewish New Year occurs in the autumn and is called Rosh Hashanah, which literally means "Head of the Year." It is also called *Yom Hazikaron*, the Day of Remembrance; *Yom Teruah*, the Day of the Sounding of the *Shofar*; and *Yom Hadin*, the Day of Judgment. Rosh Hashanah lasts for two full days, and its prayer services are marked by beautiful melodies, deep prayers, and the profound and memorable blowing of the *Shofar* (the ram's horn).

As this is the Day of Judgment, the theme of this time of year is *teshuvah*, repentance. As we close one year and begin the next, we are meant to reflect on our actions, own up to our mistakes and poor decisions, and begin the New Year with a clean slate.

There are four steps in the process of *teshuvah*, repentance: (1) Regret — consider our actions and regret our mistakes and misdeeds; (2) Stop engaging in the misdeed, for if we continue doing it, how sincere is our repentance? (3) *Vidui* — verbally confess (to G-d only) and ask for forgiveness; and finally (4) Resolve — decide clearly not to do it again, and commit to practical steps to help that happen. On Rosh Hashanah, we focus on G-d and spirituality, helping us to reestablish healthy priorities and to reconsider our actions and attitudes.

Why Judgment?

The G-d of the "Old Testament" is sometimes portrayed as angry and vengeful. Nothing could be further from the truth. By definition, G-d lacks nothing and has always lacked nothing. He created the world for us, not for Him. All of existence was brought into being out of pure love; everything we see and experience in life is here for us, and the Almighty loves us more than any human parents can love their children. So, if G-d loves us so much, why have a "Day of Judgment?" Judging seems mean!

In Jewish thought,[1] judgment is actually one of the great gifts G-d gave us. When we act badly, we bring

---

1   Based on the *Sefer Hachinuch*

negativity into our lives and the world as a whole. G-d doesn't want this negativity to hang around and take over our lives. He therefore built into the system a way to "limit the damage." By facing judgment from an Omniscient Judge, we are forced to review our deeds and deal with them. We can therefore fix our mistakes and move on, rather than having them drag us down for years to come. G-d is a G-d of love, and the judgment is a judgment coming from that love.

The Sound of the Shofar

The most famous part of Rosh Hashanah services is undoubtedly the sounding of the *Shofar*. Maimonides explains[2] that although the sounding of the *Shofar* is a Divine decree that we can never fully understand, nevertheless "we can discern a purpose in doing so. It is as if it tells us: 'Sleepers, arise from your slumber ... review your actions, repent your sins, and remember your Creator!'"[3] The *Shofar* thus serves as a type of

---

2 *Mishneh Torah, Teshuvah* 3:4

3 The great ninth-century sage Rabbi Saadia Gaon listed ten reasons for blowing the *Shofar* on Rosh Hashanah, and other commentators have added their own. Here is a brief compiled list of some of their explanations: (1) Rosh Hashanah commemorates the creation of the world and is thus described as the "coronation" of G-d. Just like a trumpet is sounded at a king's coronation, so too the *Shofar* is blown on this day. (2) The *Shofar* announces a kind of reprieve in which

spiritual alarm clock, waking us up to fundamental questions: What is life about? Why am I here? How have I been doing? How can I improve?

In blowing the *Shofar*, we make several different sounds: (1) *tekiah* is one even, long blast; (2) *shevarim*

---

we have ten more days to look into ourselves and find ways to improve and change. (3) When the Jews stood at Mt. Sinai, a great *Shofar* blared. Our *Shofar* blowing reminds us of our experience at Mt. Sinai and therefore encourages us to deepen our commitment to G-d and Judaism. (4) The *Shofar* calls out to us to improve our ways, much like the prophets called out to the Jewish People and challenged them to change. (5) In the Temple, trumpets and *Shofars* were regularly sounded. By blowing the *Shofar* we show our yearning for its rebuilding. (6) When Abraham passed his final test in the Binding of Isaac (the *Akeidah*), G-d prepared a ram in Isaac's place. By blowing a ram's horn, we recall this great merit of Abraham. (7) The *Shofar* inspires fear in the hearts of those who hear it, much like trumpets blare in battle to scare the enemy. It is the Day of Judgment and we should be afraid in order to inspire us to mend our ways, and focus on our prayers. (8) The *Shofar* reminds us of the Final Day of Judgment in the future, heralding a new world of peace, love, and spirituality. (9) The Ingathering of the Exiles will be announced with the *Shofar*, and we blow it now to focus on the unity of the Jewish People that will occur. (10) The Resurrection of the Dead will be accompanied by the sound of a *Shofar*, and we blow now to remind ourselves that just as G-d controls all life, so too does G-d control death. (11) Court sessions are often ushered in by a horn's blow; the *Shofar* ushers in this court session. We blow it ourselves to show our eagerness to be judged by G-d and our confidence in the trial's outcome.

is comprised of three medium-length wailing sounds; (3) *truah* is comprised of nine quick staccato blasts; and (4) *tekiah gedolah* is one very long, even blast.

Each set of blasts begins with the "straight" *tekiah* blasts, continues with the various "broken" blasts, and then concludes with more "straight" *tekiah* blasts, to teach us that although we started the year with vision and clarity, and often got off-track and did and said things we shouldn't have (corresponding to the "broken" sounds in the middle), we can indeed "straighten ourselves out." The sound of the *Shofar* is a sound of hope.

Beginnings

Tradition teaches that one of the most powerful things we can do on Rosh Hashanah is to use every moment of it to the fullest. While we should always endeavor to use our time productively, on Rosh Hashanah it is even more important to be constantly involved in Jewish learning, good deeds, and prayer. Anger and disagreements are to be strictly avoided. Why is this idea stressed particularly on the Jewish New Year?

Beginnings are crucial.[4] The trajectory of a projectile can change dramatically by a very small

---

4   Based on the Maharal

change in its initial launch. A boat can end up in Jakarta rather than Jerusalem if the navigation was off by even a fraction of a degree when it left port in New York. Beginnings are crucial; they establish where we are heading. On Rosh Hashanah, we do everything we can to ensure that we get off to the right start, and therefore use every moment possible to the fullest.

Declaring G-d King

Too many kings in human history have been self-proclaimed despots who were out only for their own good, or were selfish old men doing anything they could to hold on to the reins of power no matter what damage was done. In Judaism, the function of a king is to help his people live harmonious and meaningful lives.[5] Any laws he makes are for the benefit of the people, not himself. He cares about his people and does everything he can to help them. On Rosh Hashanah, then, we remind ourselves that G-d is the King of kings, the true power in the universe — and that He is a King Who cares deeply about His subjects.

Birthday of the World

We are presently in the twenty-first century since the birth of the founder of Christianity, and the

5   *Mishneh Torah*, Kings 2:6

fourteenth century since the pilgrimage of the founder of Islam. These, and many eastern religions likewise, base their calendars on the lives of their founders and the events in their particular cultural histories.

Judaism, however, bases its calendar, not on any events concerning Abraham, Sarah, Moses, or King David, but on the creation of the first sentient human beings with souls, Adam and Eve, who lived thousands of years before the first Jews. Rosh Hashanah is the birthday of humanity, for Judaism teaches and believes in the inherent value of every human being, each of which was created in "the Divine Image." The Jewish role is to model and teach about G-d, thus inspiring the entire world to fulfill its ultimate potential.

> **I Didn't Know That!**
> The Hebrew word for year, "*shanah*," is closely related to the word "*shinui*," change. So the holiday's name, Rosh Hashanah, reflects its essence: the "beginning of change."

Preparation and Practices

Elul: The entire month before Rosh Hashanah, *Elul*, is a time of focus and preparation for Rosh Hashanah and Yom Kippur. Extra prayers are said, and Jews worldwide recommit themselves to self-improvement and get ready for the High Holidays.

Prayers: The Rosh Hashanah prayers are quite unique and therefore we pray from a special prayer book called a Rosh Hashanah *Machzor*. In the period before Rosh Hashanah, special prayers known as *slichot* are said daily.

Culinary Omens (*Simanim*): We eat sweet foods (and avoid bitter ones) on Rosh Hashanah in order to express our wish that the coming year be sweet rather than bitter. The most famous example of a sweet food we eat is an apple dipped in honey. Furthermore, there is an ancient custom of eating other special foods (and saying short prayers, all of which are listed in the Rosh Hashanah prayer book) to help us focus on our wishes for the New Year. For example, one may eat a pomegranate and say, "May it be Your will ... that our merits increase as the seeds of a pomegranate."

***Hatarat Nedarim*:** During the year, a person may intentionally or unintentionally take a vow upon himself, and Jewish tradition therefore encourages us to annul these vows on the morning before Rosh Hashanah (the appropriate text is printed in the prayer books).

***Tashlich*:** On Rosh Hashanah afternoon, we perform a ceremony called *Tashlich*. We walk to a body of water (such as a river or a well) and symbolically cast our sins into the sea. The custom is based on the verse at the end of the Book of Micah: "And You will cast (*tashlich*) all their sins into the depths of the sea." Reading specific verses from the prayer book, we shake out our pockets over the water, signifying that we shed ourselves of our sins and strive for a pure heart.

White Clothing: On Rosh Hashanah, there is a custom to wear white clothing and avoid red clothing. The white clothing portrays the renewed innocence that exists after our sins have been forgiven. Also, white is the color of milk, which symbolizes sustenance and mercy. Red, on the other hand, symbolizes blood and judgment. Therefore, on Rosh Hashanah we wear white, adding to our prayers that we be judged with mercy and return to our "pure" selves. Similarly, between Rosh Hashanah and Yom Kippur, we put a white curtain on the synagogue's ark, to symbolize that our "sins will be whitened like snow."

Round Challahs: Starting with Rosh Hashanah and throughout the High Holiday season, we eat round challahs rather than the long and braided ones of a regular Shabbat or holiday. Many reasons are given for this old custom. As one year ends and the new one begins, we have "come around" like a full circle. Also, round objects have no beginning and no end, and using them during the holidays symbolizes our desire for an ongoing, continuous life full of blessings and success. Finally, some say that the roundness represents a crown, the sign of royalty, on this day of coronation of the King of kings.[6]

Tzom Gedaliah: After the destruction of the First Temple,[7] the Assyrian commanders allowed a certain amount of autonomy to the remaining Jews in Israel under the leadership of the righteous Gedaliah.[8] Gedaliah understood that, at that time, the Jewish community needed to cooperate with the occupiers. Unfortunately, some Jews were unwilling to accept any political subservience and, encouraged by jealousy and foreign influence, Yishmael son of Netaniah assassinated Gedaliah one day after Rosh Hashanah. Reprisals were quick to come. The "Fast of Gedaliah" is a "minor" fast day, observed only from sunrise to sunset. We fast not only because Gedaliah's loss was a major blow to the Jewish People, but also because

---

6   Another reason relates to beliefs of the ancient Egyptians. Egyptian polytheism (belief in many gods) was the very basis of their society and affected even the most mundane aspects of day-to-day life. For example, their bread had many corners, signifying the many different gods they worshipped. Our ancestors wanted to separate themselves from Egyptian beliefs and culture as much as possible, and so they made their bread round, signifying the unity of G-d. On Rosh Hashanah, the day we reaccept G-d as King, we emphasize this unity even through physical things such as the shape of the challahs.

7   in the sixth century BCE

8   son of Ahikam

of the tragedy that occurred in its wake: the Land of Israel was empty of Jews for the first time since we entered the land under Joshua over 800 years before.

Shabbat Shuvah: The name that is given to the Shabbat that falls between Rosh Hashanah and Yom Kippur. The name comes from the first words of the Haftorah read, *Shuvah Yisrael*, Return O Israel, as well as from the central idea of the Ten Days of Repentance, *te-shuvah*. Rabbis give special sermons to inspire congregants to improve their ways.

Rosh Hashanah Fast Facts

Name: Rosh Hashanah literally means the "Beginning of the Year," for it is the Jewish New Year.

Summary: We focus on G-d being King of the world, thus helping us establish priorities and recommit to living lives of meaning.

Timing: First and second day of *Tishrei*, in the early autumn. Lasts two full days and nights.

Questions for Discussion:[9]

1. What other names does Rosh Hashanah have? What do they mean?

2. What is the Hebrew word for "repentance"? How is it achieved?

3. If G-d loves us, why does He judge us?

4. What does the sound of the *Shofar* represent?

5. What is *Tashlich*? Does it really "remove" our sins?

6. How will you make this New Year more meaningful and joyous?

---

9   Most of these questions have numerous answers. Here are a few ideas for easy reference, to help your discussion: (1) *Yom Hazikaron*, the Day of Remembrance; *Yom Teruah*, the Day of the Sounding of the Shofar; and *Yom Hadin*, the Day of Judgment; (2) *Teshuvah*, which includes (a) regret for the deed; (b) stop doing it; (c) *vidui* — verbally confess it to G-d; and (d) resolve not to repeat it. (3) To help us deal with the past and move on to better things. (4) A wake-up call to reconsider our priorities and the "broken" parts of our lives. (5) We symbolically cast our sins into the water, but the real removal of sin occurs through *teshuvah*. (6) Rosh Hashanah is the anniversary of the day the world (really, humanity) was created. On this day, all of Creation renews itself. On this day, we too can renew ourselves.

Chapter 2:
Yom Kippur

"For on this day shall atonement be made for you, to cleanse you; from all your sins shall you be clean before the Lord."

(Leviticus 16:30)

Yom Kippur, literally the "Day of Atonement," helps us atone for our sins. It is also known as *Yom Hadin*, the Day of Judgment, for on it we are judged by G-d for our actions. Yom Kippur occurs on the tenth day of the Hebrew month of *Tishrei*, ten days from Rosh Hashanah, in the early autumn, and lasts just over twenty-four hours.

Yom Kippur is often described as the holiest day of the Jewish year. It helps atone for our sins and allows us to start the year fresh "with a clean slate." The theme of our prayers is regret and repentance before G-d's judgment. In order to help us focus on the tasks at hand, as well as remind us of our weakness and dependence on G-d, on this unique day we "afflict" ourselves through five commandments: (1) not to eat or drink; (2) not to wash; (3) not to wear leather shoes;[10] (4) not to have intimate relations; and (5) not to anoint ourselves with oils.

Yom Kippur is a gift from G-d. On this one day, if we regret our actions and repent, all of our sins will be forgiven and we can start anew. Considering how long it may have taken to commit all these acts, it is truly incredible that one day's resolve can wipe the slate clean. G-d wanted to make sure that we correctly use this great window of opportunity and so added these "prohibitions" to help us focus.

How do they help us focus? Physical pleasures tend to strengthen our non-spiritual sides. During the year, we lead lives of balance, trying to infuse spirituality into our regular physical lives and thus uplift them. On this one day, however, we turn our

---

10　Surrounding the lowest part of our bodies and allowing them to function, shoes represent our physicality. Accordingly, at times when physicality can block a spiritual connection, G-d commands us to remove our shoes. Moses was commanded to remove his shoes at the Burning Bush, and Joshua was so commanded when being addressed by an angel. The priests (Kohanim) in the Temple would be barefoot, and even today they remove their shoes whenever they give the priestly blessing. On this holiest of days, we rise above our physicality and reach into the heavens, minus the shoes. Why leather? Firstly, leather represents wealth and materialism and so is most at odds with the spirit of the day. Secondly, leather comes from (formerly) living animals, and thus is the full expression of physicality.

backs on physicality completely in order to resemble angels (who are completely nonphysical). By reaching for this exalted state, even though we can't stay there, we hope to concentrate fully, achieve atonement, and start the year letting our souls shine through for the rest of the year.

Judgment Day

The judgment of Yom Kippur is a critical part of the day and a crucial component of our Jewish lives. Educators and sociologists tell us that a lack of discipline can sometimes be more damaging than an overabundance of it. A child can too easily get the message that no one cares about his actions and thus that no one cares about him. Defined rules and limits give the clear message that although we may not always see things eye to eye, what you do *does* matter to me. *You* matter to me. The same is true with G-d. Our actions have meaning and consequences. There is Someone Who cares. How we conduct our lives matters. *We* matter.

G-d cares deeply about us. He knows that we are human and make mistakes. He therefore gave us Yom Kippur to pause, reflect, and apologize before moving ahead. The Torah tells us to *"Purify yourselves before G-d"* (Leviticus 16:30) at this time of year. In Hebrew, "repentance" is called *teshuvah*, which literally means to return, i.e., turn away from our mistakes and turn back to G-d.

We do this by confessing our sins to G-d directly. Judaism does not believe in confession to another human being. Each of us can and should speak to G-d directly, with no intermediaries. Why not just rely on a general "I'm sorry" to cover everything? By taking a few moments to contemplate our various areas of success and failure, we are forced to realize what our faults are and where we need work. This realization is the first step in the process of change, for we can then be on the lookout for future pitfalls and hopefully avoid them.

Note that if we wronged another person, apologizing to G-d isn't enough; we need to apologize and appease the person we offended or hurt as well. And we should forgive others of anything they may have done against us. Furthermore, note that part of true repentance is the resolution to change our behavior. On Yom Kippur, we should resolve to be nicer to people, to be more sensitive to their situations, and to try and find firm ways of doing so.

Eating, Fasting, and Physicality

Yom Kippur occurs on the tenth day of the Hebrew month of *Tishrei*. The Talmud teaches that anyone who eats on the day before Yom Kippur (the ninth of *Tishrei*) "is considered as if he fasted on the ninth and tenth," meaning that eating is considered as meritorious as fasting! And indeed, as mentioned above, it is a mitzvah to eat before the fast starts. But why is eating so meritorious? What is so hard about eating?

Judaism is not an ascetic religion. Our leaders are not celibate; a normal marital life doesn't contradict holiness. Similarly, the Jewish ideal is not solitary meditation on a mountaintop. We are supposed to live in communities and help each other. Spirituality comes through connecting to others, not by disassociating ourselves from them, and by uplifting the physical, not by denying it.

Eating *before* Yom Kippur is thus important so that we remember that the *fasting* of Yom Kippur is not the Jewish ideal. Denial of the physical is sometimes necessary, but using the physical for the right purposes is equally powerful in helping us become spiritual human beings.

Holiday of Responsibility

"But your Honor, my client grew up ..."

Western society today struggles with the concept of responsibility. Criminals blame their acts on poverty and lack of education. Husbands blame their infidelities on biological urges. While these factors certainly make life challenging, we should not ignore the fact that many people from the exact same backgrounds and in the exact same situations choose not to murder, cheat, or commit other crimes. It is certainly easier to blame external forces for our mistakes — it takes maturity, though, to admit mistakes and say, "I did it. I was wrong. I'm sorry and I'm going to do better in the future."

Yom Kippur is the holiday of responsibility. If those words (holiday and responsibility) sound like an oxymoron, be careful — you may have fallen into the trap. By taking responsibility for our actions, we can achieve completeness and happiness. The past doesn't have to drag us down, because we are mature enough to deal with it. I am not perfect. I have done such and such. But I admit it. I take responsibility and vow to change.

Even the afflictions of Yom Kippur relate to its theme of responsibility. For example, by fasting, we show that we are capable of controlling our eating. By not drinking, we show that we can control our drinking.

By not having marital relations, we show that we are in control of our intimate lives. By turning all of these pleasures "off" for one day a year, we remind ourselves that we are also in control of them when they are "on." By taking responsibility for our weaknesses and faults, we are able move beyond them. With the power of Yom Kippur, the slate can be wiped clean and we can truly move on. What a gift! What a holiday!

> **I didn't know that!**
> The word for sin in Hebrew is *chet*, which means to err or to miss. The same word also refers to an arrow, as in when an archer misses the target. The implication is that all sins are really mistakes. And like an archer who misses the target, we should try to learn from our mistakes and do a little better next time!

Preparation and Practices[11]

The Ten Days of Awe: This period of time

---

11   Here are some other customs of Yom Kippur:
   Mikveh: Some immerse themselves in a *mikveh* (ritual bath) on Erev Yom Kippur.
   Tefillah Zakkah: literally "the pure prayer," said upon entry to synagogue before Kol Nidre.
   Kapparot: During the days preceding Yom Kippur, some take a rooster (for a man) or a chicken (for a woman) and say special *kapparot* prayers as the fowl is turned above one's head. Symbolizing the judgment of the upcoming day, it is a method of awakening us to repentance. The bird goes to feed

from Rosh Hashanah to Yom Kippur is a time of introspection and self-improvement. We give charity generously during this period, and apologize to anyone we may have offended during the preceding year.

Eating on Erev Yom Kippur: It is considered an actual mitzvah to eat and drink well on the day before the fast of Yom Kippur. The last meal before the fast begins is called the *Seudah Hamafseket* and must be finished well before sunset, leaving enough time left to get to shul for …

Kol Nidre: Possibly the most famous prayer of the Jewish year, the Kol Nidre service occurs as Yom Kippur begins. Its haunting melody has touched Jewish hearts for generations. Its words actually refer to nullifying oaths and vows. While not affecting business commitments, what we say does relate to ritual practices, and teaches how seriously we are to take our words.

Vidui: This literally means confession, reciting out loud the sins that we have committed.

White clothing: We wear white clothing as a symbol of cleanliness from sin. It is not appropriate

the poor, and many today use money instead of an actual bird.

Books: A rare but beautiful custom is to place books of Jewish learning on the table instead of plates, emphasizing that our "food" on this day is comprised of study and contemplation.

to wear any ostentatious dress or jewelry, or to display our wealth on this Day of Judgment.

Yizkor: Literally "remembrance," *Yizkor* is the the memorial prayer said for the souls of the deceased. It is said in shul on Pesach, Shavuot, Yom Kippur, and Shemini Azteret. According to Ashkenazic custom, children with both parents alive leave shul during this short prayer. In memory of deceased loved ones, we give charity and light *yahrtzeit* candles well before sundown and let them burn throughout the holiday.

The Kohen Gadol: The High Priest represented the entire Jewish People when he entered the holiest place on earth — the inner sanctuary of the Temple — on this day, the holiest day of the year. During Temple times, he was at the center of a beautiful and meaningful ceremony on Yom Kippur; today, we recount this service (*avodah*) in our prayers.

The Book of Jonah: This is read on this day, discussing how the inhabitants of Nineveh were saved when they repented, thus inspiring us to do the same.

The Neilah prayer: Said at the end of Yom Kippur, Neilah represents the "closing of the gates." This beautiful prayer helps us focus on repentance, forgiveness, and change in the last moments of this awesome day.

Yom Kippur Fast Facts

Name: Yom Kippur literally means the Day of Atonement, when we can gain atonement for our sins and start anew.

Summary: We fast and pray on this holiest day of the year as atonement for the wrongs we've committed, and to help us focus on self-improvement and introspection. Commandments include not eating, drinking, washing, having intimate relations, wearing leather shoes, and anointing oneself with oils.

Timing: Tenth day of *Tishrei*, ten days from Rosh Hashanah, in the early autumn. Lasts just over twenty-four hours.

Questions for Discussion:[12]

1. Why does Rosh Hashanah come before Yom Kippur?

2. Why do we wear white on Yom Kippur?

3. How does the prohibition of wearing leather shoes fit into the themes of Yom Kippur?

4. Jewish holidays generally correspond to historical events. Which historical event does Yom Kippur correspond to?

5. What kind of sins does Yom Kippur NOT atone for?

6. Why is the book of Jonah read on Yom Kippur?

---

12 Many answers can be offered to these questions. Here are a few ideas to help your discussion. (1) If we do not realize that G-d runs the world, we cannot properly repent. Only when we remind ourselves of our Creator can we reconsider our actions and judge whether they were appropriate or not. (2) To symbolize "cleansing" ourselves of sin, and to resemble angels who do not eat or drink. (3) Shoes, especially leather ones, represent pure physicality and on this day we are trying to raise ourselves up and reach heights of spirituality. (4) After the sin of the Golden Calf, the first tablets were smashed. On this day, Moses came down from Mt. Sinai with the second set of Tablets, thus establishing the day as the symbol of forgiveness. (5) Offenses to other people — we need to ask their forgiveness first. (6) So we will be inspired by the repentance of the people of Nineveh.

Chapter 3:
Sukkot

"You shall dwell in Sukkot seven days, every citizen in Israel shall dwell in Sukkot, so that your descendants shall know that in Sukkot I caused the Children of Israel to dwell when I brought them out of Egypt."

(Leviticus 23:42,43)

Sukkot, literally the festival of the "booths," derives its name from the temporary, hut-like dwellings we live in during the holiday, which commemorate the booths[13] the Jews lived in as they wandered in the desert. This eight-day-long festival occurs five days after Yom Kippur and is also called *Chag Ha'asif*, The Harvest Festival, for it occurs in the fall, at harvest time.

The most famous symbols of the holiday are the *Sukkot* themselves. Sukkot consist of walls and cut tree branches (or special reed mats) as cover. Children

---

Or, alternatively, the Clouds of Glory

love making and decorating the *Sukkah*.[14] It doesn't take them long to learn how to build it better and more quickly than their parents! There are wonderful meals eaten in the *Sukkah*, with singing, happiness, and enjoying time with the family. Sukkot is a time of genuine heartfelt celebration. Joy is so important to the holiday that if it rains, we are meant to leave the *Sukkah* — because this beautiful mitzvah is intended to cause us happiness, not distress.

The second most characteristic aspect of the holiday is the mitzvah of bringing together the Four Species (palm branch, citron, myrtle, and willow) and shaking them. We wave them in all directions to show that G-d is everywhere. The fragrant smell and beautiful picture they create is most remarkable.

The Four Species

One of the loveliest of all Jewish "rites" is that of the Four Species, whose color and scent provide a wonderful experience. The Torah tells us to take *"the fruits of a pleasant tree, and palm branches, and thick leafy boughs, and willows of the brook, and rejoice before your Lord, G-d"* (Leviticus 23:40). The *etrog*, the fruit

---

14   Man says to a Rabbi, "Gee Rabbi, I like being Jewish and all, but why can't Jews have a Christmas tree? Look how much the kids love decorating it and look forward to it all year." Rabbi responds, "Hey Jerry, have you ever heard of Sukkot?"

of the pleasant tree, is a fragrant yellow citron fruit native to Israel, and the thick boughs are myrtles. The *etrog* is taken in the left hand and the other three species are taken together in the right hand. All four are thus brought together and shaken in all directions.

There is much symbolism[15] to the Four Species. The *etrog* has both taste and smell, representing Jews with both Torah learning and good deeds. The *lulav*, the palm branch, has taste (its dates taste delicious) but no smell, representing those with Torah learning but no good deeds. The myrtle (*hadas*) has scent but no taste, representing those with good deeds but no Torah. Finally, the willow (*aravah*) has neither taste nor smell, representing Jews lacking both Torah learning and good deeds. On Sukkot, all four come together

---

15 Also, the *Sefer Hachinuch* explains that the Four Species resemble some human organs. The *etrog* resembles the heart, "the seat of the intelligence," teaching that we should serve G-d with our hearts, and minds. The *lulav* resembles the spine, teaching that we should use our entire bodies in serving G-d. The myrtle's leaves resemble eyes, teaching that we should not let our eyes lead us astray. And the willow's leaves resemble lips, teaching that we must be careful with our words. At a mystical level, the Four Species look like letters of G-d's Name (*Yud-Heh-Vav-Heh*). The *etrog* resembles the *yud*, the curving myrtle the *heh*, the *lulav* the *vav*, and the bent willow the final *heh*. By bringing the *lulav* bundle together, we are bringing G-d's Name together and helping to reestablish the fundamental unity of the universe.

in one beautiful bundle, showing that true service of G-d requires true unity among all Jews. If one of the species is missing, the entire bundle is invalid.

Cultivating Happiness

We move out of our air-conditioned, comfortable houses into flimsy little booths. And the great mitzvah of the day is "to rejoice in our festival." Many have asked, how is "roughing it" for a week supposed to make us happy? As we all realize, there are wealthy people who are happy and wealthy people who are unhappy. There are poor people who are happy and poor people who are unhappy. The point is that while material comforts can certainly make life easier and more pleasant, in the end happiness does not come from external things, but rather it comes from a sense of meaning in life and a positive internal attitude.

This is why Sukkot occurs at the time of gathering in the crops, for it is precisely in times of abundance that we are likely to feel that material wealth is the key to a happy life. The Torah therefore instructs us to move out of the physical comfort of our homes, reminding us that in the end it is G-d Who protects us, and it is the relationships, meaning, and spirituality in our lives that provide our true happiness.

Ushpizin

There is a tradition in Jewish mystical texts that on each day of the holiday, seven special guests (*Ushpizin* in Aramaic) visit the *Sukkah*, each taking their turn at leading the way. The guests are Abraham, Isaac, Jacob, Joseph, Moses, Aron, and David. What is their specific connection to Sukkot?

Interestingly, all of them left their homes: Abraham left Ur Casdim and came to what would eventually be called Israel. Isaac moved to the land of the Philistines (the *Plishtim*). Jacob fled to Aram. Joseph was sold into slavery to Egypt. Moses fled to Midian. Aron wandered in the desert for forty years with the nation and never entered Israel. David escaped to Gat and Moab. Their exiles were difficult, but all of them became stronger from the experience and gained clarity on what is truly important in life. On Sukkot, when we are "exiled" from our homes to live in temporary shelters, we are "visited" by our ancestors who were also exiled in order to be inspired by them.

I didn't know that!

The name of the holiday, Sukkot, is related to the word *soche* or "to see." Living in a *Sukkah* enables us to see what is really important: meaning, family, and spirituality.

Preparations and Practices

Building *Sukkot*: Ideally begun immediately following the termination of Yom Kippur, building and decorating the *Sukkah* is a fun, hands-on experience for the whole family. Some use wood planks and cut palm (or other kinds of) tree branches. Nowadays, easy-to-assemble *Sukkah* kits can be ordered online, including everything you need. Many decorate the *Sukkah* with pictures of Israel, the special Seven Species of Israel[16] (figs, dates, wheat, barley, grapes, pomegranates, and olives), drawings and pictures with Jewish themes, or anything cute the children make!

Buy Four Species: In the weeks before Sukkot, Jews around the world begin searching for the Four Species, with the most desired specimens judged by both their beauty and by their *kashrus* — to meet the requirements of Jewish law. Nowadays, sets can be ordered online or through most synagogues.

***Simchat Beit Hashoevah*:** When the Temple stood, in the evenings of the holiday, multitudes of men and women would come together in the Temple courtyard to watch the greatest sages of the time dance and celebrate in the *Simchat Beit Hashoevah*, the rejoicing of the Water-Drawing. Two thousand years ago, the Chief Rabbi of the entire Jewish People,

---

16   Many try to eat the Seven Species during the festival as well.

Rabbi Shimon ben Gamliel, would juggle torches and perform gymnastic feats. Huge golden candlesticks were placed in the Temple courtyard and could be seen for tremendous distances. The Talmud teaches that whoever did not witness this, "never saw a celebration."[17] Today, the week of Sukkot is still filled with *Simchat Beit Hashoevah* parties complete with dancing and singing.

***Hoshanahs* and Hoshanah Rabbah:** During the week of Sukkot, part of the prayer service includes circling the *bimah* (Torah lectern) while holding the Four Species. The last day of Sukkot is called Hoshanah Rabbah, and on this day seven circles are made. *Hoshanah Rabbah* is a special day with festive meals, and one of its customs is the taking of willow twigs and beating them on the ground.

Read the Book of Ecclesiastes (Kohelet): During the holiday, we publicly read the Book of Ecclesiastes, which was written by King Solomon. The wisest of all men, Solomon, writes that he has achieved all that man can achieve — great wealth, wisdom, fame, many wives, etc. — and yet he concludes that in the end, "all is vanity." In the end, physicality and materialism are limited. The only things that really last are our *mitzvot* — our good deeds and spiritual

17   *Sukkah* 51a

acts. We read this book during Sukkot to remind us that even though the harvest is in and material wealth abounds, we should remember that life is about spirituality and goodness, not money.

Sukkot Fast Facts

Name: Sukkot literally means "booths" or "huts," for we dwell in temporary booths for the duration of the holiday.

Summary: We eat and sleep (if warm enough) in the *Sukkah*, celebrating with family and friends throughout the holiday. We also wave the Four Species.

Timing: Fifteenth day of *Tishrei*, five days after Yom Kippur, in the early autumn. Lasts for eight days.

Questions for Discussion:[18]

1. Why does Yom Kippur come before Sukkot?
2. On Sukkot Jews would visit Jerusalem on a pilgrimage. What other two holidays did this occur on?
3. Name the Four Species.
4. What parallels do Sukkot and Passover have?
5. What do Sukkot and Chanukah have in common?
6. Why is the Book of Ecclesiastes read on Sukkot?

---

18   Many answers can be offered to these questions. Here are a few ideas to help your discussion. (1) When a person takes responsibility for his actions and achieves atonement, one can truly rejoice! (2) Passover and Shavuot (3) Citron (*etrog*), palm branch (*lulav*), myrtle (*hadas*), and willow (*aravah*). (4) They both occur on the fifteenth of the Hebrew month, exactly half a year apart, and last for eight days. They both focus on our leaving Egypt. Can you think of any more parallels? (5) They are both eight days long, they are both Kohen-connected, for Sukkot's clouds were in the merit of Aron the High Priest, and the saviors of Chanukah were Kohanim. Furthermore, on both holidays many beautify the ritual objects used (the *Sukkah*, *etrog* holder, and Menorah). Finally, the last day of each has extra importance, *Hoshanah Rabbah* and *Zot Chanukah*. (6) To remind us that spirituality is more important than materialism.

Chapter 4:
Shemini Atzeret and Simchat Torah

"Rejoice on your festival."

(Deuteronomy 16:14)

Simchat Torah, literally the "joy of the Torah," is one of the happiest days of the Jewish year. We read the last portion of the Torah, at the end of Deuteronomy, and begin the first portion, at the beginning of Genesis. This completion and new beginning are cause for celebration, and celebrate we certainly do!

Most synagogues remove all the Torah scrolls from the Holy Ark. They are then carried joyfully around the *bimah* (Torah lectern) in the center of the sanctuary. Adults and children sing, dance, and rejoice. In many congregations, a large *tallit* (prayer shawl) is spread over the heads of children as they are called to the Torah together. Children in particular look forward to the celebrations and often dance with flags. Simchat Torah needs to be experienced to be more fully appreciated. Chasidic congregations have been described as attaining "exalted frenzy," while

German Jewish synagogues are more known for their elegant songs and dances. Wherever you celebrate, though, the underlying feelings are the same — the joy of being a Jew.

Because Shemini Atzeret, literally "the gathering of the eighth[19] [day]," immediately follows Sukkot, it

19 The Maharal of Prague is well known for his explanations of what the different numbers represent. For our purposes, let us start with the number seven. The number seven is best represented by a cube, which has six sides and one center point, adding up to seven. Similarly, there are six directions: up and down, front and back, and left and right, in addition to the center starting point. There are also seven days in a week and seven notes on a music scale. The number seven represents the completion, the full picture of the natural, physical world. If seven represents the natural world, what does eight represent? Eight is the first stage beyond seven, and thus represents the metaphysical (literally, beyond the physical) phenomena that exist outside of normal, natural constraints. *Brit milah* thus occurs on the eighth day; it is a religious and spiritual act performed upon the physical body. In other words, eight reaches beyond physical norms and limitations for higher goals and aspirations. Shemini Atzeret is another example of this concept. After the "natural" celebration of Sukkot, we have one more day of reaching beyond into the metaphysical. Unlike Sukkot, Shemini Atzeret is just for the Jewish People — a metaphysical number for a metaphysical People. When the Talmud says that there is no *mazal* to the Jews, it means that we are not bound by natural laws or even astrological principles. Dozens of powerful empires have attempted to destroy us, yet we have not only survived but held onto our religion, our language, and have

is easy to think that it is part of the Sukkot holiday itself, while in reality it is its own separate festival.[20] Evidence of this independence is the fact that on Shemini Atzeret, the *Sukkah* is not used and the Four Species are not taken. G-d is sad, so to speak, that the holidays are over[21] and the national visits to Jerusalem have ended. Knowing that we will be missed like any

---

made an unprecedented return to our land after a grueling 2,000-year exile. Mark Twain perhaps said it best when he asked, "All things remain mortal but the Jew; all other forces pass, but he remains. What is the secret of his immortality?" We are a miracle People, and it is most fitting that this eighth day is focused on a unique People that goes beyond normal limitations.

20   Sukkot occurs on the fifteenth of the month and so does Passover. Sukkot lasts seven days and so does Passover. Sukkot has a one-day holiday after it (Shemini Atzeret) with no particular rituals and ... so does Passover (it is called Shavuot!). In the Torah, both Shemini Atzeret and Shavuot are referred to as an *Atzeret* meaning a gathering. Symmetry would indicate that just like we need seven weeks to get ready for the big day of Shavuot, so too we need seven weeks to get ready for the big day of Shemini Atzeret. And it would have been that way, the Talmud tells us, except that G-d let us have the festival immediately after Sukkot so that we did not have to travel to Jerusalem another time during the winter rain and mud.

21   Sukkot, as explained by the *Sefer Hachinuch*, is the last Biblical holiday of the Jewish calendar (having already passed through Passover, Shavuot, Rosh Hashanah, and Yom Kippur).

children leaving home, G-d asks us[22] to "stay one more day" and join together in the holiday of Shemini Atzeret. In this way, Shemini Atzeret is in a sense "G-d's final hug of the year." Knowing this, it becomes clear why there are no particular commandments on Shemini Atzeret (as compared to the *Sukkah*, matzah, *Shofar*, etc. of other holidays): it is the final holiday of the High Holiday season, a day for basking in G-d's presence and enjoying our Jewishness. These two days, combined into one in Israel, take place in the autumn, immediately following Sukkot.

Loving Learning

The Torah is read in a yearly cycle so that we review it all every year and keep its lessons fresh in our minds. The cycle begins at the beginning of the calendar year just after Rosh Hashanah so that we have a new beginning at a time of new beginnings. We finish the old cycle and start the new cycle on the very same day. Why? Why not just conclude the previous cycle at the

---

22   Sukkot is a universalistic holiday, with seventy offerings being brought on behalf of the seventy prototype nations of the world. On Shemini Atzeret, the final holiday of the holiday season, the only offering brought was a lone bull on behalf of the Jewish People — for this day is just for us, a final hug for G-d's most devoted children before they return home for the winter.

end of the previous year and start the new cycle at the beginning of the new year? We start immediately after we finish in order to emphasize that we aren't happy the Torah is over. Rather, we can't wait to start learning again.

Simchat Torah in the Soviet Union

After decades of systematic Soviet attempts to wipe out all traces of Jewish knowledge and practice from the Jews within the Soviet Union, Soviet Jews were galvanized by news of the miraculous Israeli victory over massive Arab armies in 1967. New pride surged in their Jewish identities. This new Soviet Jewish pride was expressed in many ways. Underground Hebrew classes were held as well as lectures on Jewish religion and history. And, courageously, young Soviet Jews began to celebrate Simchat Torah joyfully, in full public view of Soviet intelligence and police authorities. Their celebration was a clear statement: "Try as you might, you cannot take away our Jewish pride and devotion!" Crowds at these public celebrations reached the tens of thousands. Today, wherever there are concentrations of Russian Jews, Simchat Torah is particularly joyful and meaningful.

Yom Kippur versus Simchat Torah

In our times, unfortunately, Judaism has often been reduced to a handful of boring rituals fulfilled out of a sense of obligation rather than joy at being Jewish. People don't understand their Bar/Bat Mitzvah portions, can't wait for the High Holiday prayers to end, and race through the *Haggadah* in order to get to the food. Sadly, the peace and joy of Judaism have been largely lost. One prime example of this is Shabbat, the holiday of holidays whose singing and togetherness would do more for Jewish continuity than any Sunday school possibly could. Other examples are Sukkot and Simchat Torah; those who only frequent synagogue on the High Holidays get a rather imbalanced view of Judaism. Rosh Hashanah and Yom Kippur are serious days, and indeed life should not be taken too lightly. However, Sukkot and Simchat Torah occur immediately after the High Holidays in order to emphasize that being Jewish is more than obligations. We also need to sing, dance, laugh, and celebrate.

> **I Didn't Know That!**
>
> The Jewish calendar has many parallels. Sukkot starts in the middle of the month and has an eighth day, Shemini Atzeret, attached to it. Exactly six months later, Passover starts in the middle of the month and has an eighth day, Shavuot, attached to it through the counting of the Omer.

Simchat Torah and Shemini Atzeret Fast Facts

Name: The name Simchat Torah literally means "joy of the Torah." The name Shemini Atzeret means the "eighth day of gathering."

Summary: Simchat Torah is a day of celebration of the Torah. We dance and sing around the synagogue. Shemini Atzeret is a day of gathering together and celebrating the joy of being Jewish.

Timing: The twenty-second and twenty-third of *Tishrei*, in the autumn immediately following Sukkot.

Questions for Discussion:[23]

1. What do the names of the holidays mean?
2. What is the theme of Simchat Torah?
3. What is theme of Shemini Atzeret?
4. Why does Shemini Atzeret occur at this time of year?
5. Why do we begin the Torah reading now?
6. Do we live in the *Sukkah* for these holidays?

---

23   Many answers exist. Here are a few ideas to get you talking: (1) The name Simchat Torah literally means "joy of the Torah," the name Shemini Atzeret means the "eighth day of gathering." (2) Joy of the Torah (3) One last day of being together with G-d during the holidays (4) Right after Sukkot, one last day at the end of the holiday season (5) Immediately upon finishing it, we start again emphasizing how much we love learning Torah. (6) No — they are independent holidays.

Chapter 5:
Chanukah

"No other two races have set such a mark upon the world. Each of them, from angles so different, has left us with the inheritance of its genius and wisdom. No two cities have counted more with mankind than Athens and Jerusalem."

(Sir Winston Churchill)

After the death of Alexander the Great[24] in the year 323 BCE, the entire Middle East was divided among his successors. A general named Antiochus eventually took control of Israel. One fact about him gives a good sense of the kind of ruler he was: Antiochus added the title of "Epiphanes" to his name because it means "G-d made manifest" — he literally felt he was G-d. Our

---

24 It was the successors of Alexander the Great who oppressed us, but while he was alive, our relationship to the Greek superpower was a good one. Alexander himself showed great reverence for the Jewish sages, bowing his head when he met Shimon Hatzaddik, who was the leader of the Jewish People at the time. Alexander was so favorably looked upon that for a whole year after his death, every Jewish baby boy was named Alexander after him, and Alexander remains a "Jewish" name to this day.

Jewish ancestors did not lack a sense of humor; we referred to him as Antiochus Epimanes — Antiochus the Madman.

Antiochus and his fellow Greeks wanted the whole world to adopt their beliefs. When the Jews showed little interest in abandoning their heritage, the Greeks and their Hellenist (Greek-cultured) Jewish helpers tried to "modernize" us by force. They outlawed the practice of Judaism and study of Torah and built a gymnasium right next to the Temple, aiming to sway the masses to Greek ideals. Eventually they placed an idolatrous statue of Zeus in the Temple itself. Monthly sacrifices to their gods were brought in the Temple, "sacred" prostitution was introduced, and pigs were brought on the altar — just to name a few of the changes they introduced.

The pious Mattityahu Chashmonai moved to the rural Modi'in area in order to avoid these Greek influences, but within a short period of time the Greek threat spread throughout all of Israel. Greek soldiers arrived in his village one day and demanded that the inhabitants sacrifice a pig to their pagan god. Mattityahu stood up to the Greeks and their Jewish collaborators, fled with his sons, and together they became the leaders of a Jewish guerilla army fighting for the preservation of Judaism. When Mattityahu died, his son Judah the Maccabee took over, leading us to victory. The title Maccabee means "the hammer," or alternatively it is an acronym of M-K-B-A, *Mi Kamocha BeElim Adon-nai,* "Who is like You among the gods, O Lord" — the verse emblazoned on Judah's banner.

On the twenty-fifth day of the Hebrew month of *Kislev,* in the middle of winter, Judah Maccabee's forces recaptured the Temple and began rededicating it to the service of G-d. When the Hasmoneans (also known as the Maccabees) defeated the Greeks and arrived in the Temple, they tried to relight the ancient seven-branched Menorah housed inside. Finding only enough kosher oil for one day, they lit what they had anyway and miraculously it lasted eight days, giving them enough time to produce more. The very next year, our sages declared the days of the miracle to be a festival, celebrating our victory over the Greeks and the miracle of the oil. In the middle of the long, dark winter, Chanukah provides much needed inspiration, joy, family time, and fun. The main mitzvah is lighting the Chanukah candles every night for eight nights.

Names of the Holiday

The name Chanukah, sometimes spelled Hanukkah, refers to the rededication of the Temple by the Maccabees, but also has several other connotations.[25]

---

25   The name can also refer to another dedication (*Chanukah*):

The Maccabees rested (*chanu* in Hebrew) from their battle on the twenty-fifth day of the month of *Kislev*, the date of Chanukah today. In Hebrew, the number twenty-five is written with the letters *chof-heh*, the last two letters of the word Chanukah in Hebrew. Also, the word *chein*, making up the other letters in the word Chanukah, denotes grace, alluding to the fact that the Jewish warriors found Divine "grace" on the twenty-fifth of *Kislev*.

The word Chanukah is also related to the word for education, *chinuch*; both "education" and "dedication" refer to setting the foundations of something. For this reason, many have the custom of meeting at this time of year to discuss and improve Jewish education in their communities.

Finally, the holiday is sometimes referred to as the Festival of Lights, due to the candles that are lit.

The Message of Chanukah

Chanukah is sometimes portrayed as a struggle for religious tolerance, based on the fact that the Greeks

---

that of the Tabernacle, which occurred at almost the same time of the year during the forty years in the desert over 1,000 years before the Maccabean revolt. Although the Tabernacle was physically ready at this time, G-d decided to wait until the month of *Nissan* to dedicate it. Thus G-d "repaid the loss" to the month of *Kislev* with the "Chanukah" of the Hasmoneans.

outlawed our religion and we struggled to be able to practice it. Alternatively, Chanukah is portrayed as a fight for national independence, based on the fact that a Jewish militia fought the powerful Greek army. Both of these explanations are true to a certain extent, but miss the essence of Chanukah.

The real enemy of the Maccabees was not Greek military might. When the Greek army arrived in Israel, there was no resistance. Opposition only began later when the Greeks revealed their desire to dispose of Judaism and replace it with universal Greek ideals. The essence of Chanukah is neither religious pluralism nor independence, but the very survival of Judaism. This holiday more than any other celebrates the survival of Judaism over the forces of assimilation.

Greek Decrees

The Greeks felt they had a mission to fill the world with Greek culture and civilization. Those who would not willingly join them on their "march forward into the future" were targeted for conquer and forced "conversion" to their beliefs. It is important to note that the Greeks did not want to physically destroy the Jewish People. The Greeks very much desired the whole world — and especially the Jews — join in their worldview. In order to wean us from our "archaic" religion, they outlawed what they perceived as the most powerful parts of Judaism.

The first of these was Shabbat. As the beginning of the Book of Genesis describes, Jews rest on the seventh day just as G-d rested on it after creating the world. Shabbat declares that we believe in G-d as Creator of the world, and strengthens Jewish community and beliefs. The Greeks believed that the world had always existed, that there was no Creation and certainly no Creator, and therefore they outlawed Shabbat

The second mitzvah the Greeks had in their sights was circumcision. Circumcision declares that the human body, and by extension human character, needs to be improved. It teaches that human beings are not perfect, and that physicality is not the primary value in life. In doing so, circumcision directly opposes the Greek view of the perfection of the human body and by extension the perfection and centrality of the human being — the notion that formed the basis of their culture. Furthermore, circumcision declared us to be a unique, particularistic people unwilling to disappear into the majority culture. For these reasons, the Greeks outlawed circumcision.

The third mitzvah the Greeks targeted was the sanctification of the New Moon, Rosh Chodesh. The Supreme Jewish Court would declare the new month based on testimony of the moon's early appearance. This system showed that we are not simply "victims" of astrology, fights between the gods, or random occurrence. Rather, human actions count; *we* determine the new moon and thus the holiday schedule. We can affect the universe in an "upwards" kind of motion. Human beings have enormous power, and are responsible for their actions. The Greeks believed in a series of gods who affected us in a downward kind of motion — that our physical world had no effect on the Divine. They therefore outlawed the Sanctification of the New Moon.

But finally, and above all, the Greeks also commanded us to stop studying Torah. They knew that authentic Torah study is the spine of the Jewish People. With it, Jews become excited and knowledgeable about their heritage. Without it, as contemporary statistics show, our grandchildren will simply not be identifiable as Jews, and a 3,000-year-old family tradition will be lost. The Greeks wanted us to disappear as Jews, and so outlawed the fundamental and most crucial method of keeping a Jewish identity — Torah study. From our point of view, the lesson is clear: Jewish knowledge is the key to our survival.

The Problem with the Greeks

In large measure, modern Western civilization

traces itself to the very same Greek civilization that our ancestors fought against. The Greeks (and their successors, the Romans) gave the world philosophy, sports, theater, poetry, architecture, and especially democracy. It is no coincidence that the United States Capitol building is of Greek architectural design; the democratic form of government it represents originated in Greece. All these contributions seem very positive, and both Greek and Jewish culture shared admiration of the mind. The Greeks were, after all, much more advanced than the barbarians surrounding them. Why did the Jews resist Greek progress? What were our ancestors afraid of?

One explanation relates to the reality of Greek civilization. Notwithstanding its beautiful outward trappings, Greek society was not something to be admired. For reasons such as deformity, expense, or gender (boys preferred, girls not), babies were commonly murdered by leaving them outside to starve to death, and pedophilia was the accepted norm.[26]

---

26 As Michael Grant writes in *The Founders of the Western World: a History of Greece and Rome* (Scribners, 1991, p.16): "In most Greek communities the women were kept at home, and men spent their days with other men or boys. Artists paid special attention to the nude masculine form; and pederasty [inappropriate relationships with children] abounded ... and indeed a whole philosophy was built up around the pederastic situation, founded on the concept that the ... [adult] was the

The Greek greats such as Sophocles and Plato were all involved in inappropriate relationships of this type — today rightly considered a terrible crime!

But the Jewish opposition to Greek culture went even deeper than being repulsed by its negative aspects. The Jews of the time objected to the Greek philosophy of being separate from G-d. The Jews of the time realized that without a clear objective basis for morality, Greek literature and philosophy was of little value, because without G-d's guiding hand and commandments, philosophy could justify any cruelty.

We learned this lesson again in the middle of the twentieth century. Germany was by far the most enlightened, cultured, and progressive culture in the world, and yet it gave birth to Nazism. The history of Greece and Germany remind us that literature and philosophy absent of G-d are really not so impressive.

Greek Beauty versus Jewish Beauty

Many museums today have examples of ancient Greek statues, most of which depict the human body. The ancient Greeks worshipped the human form and sought to replicate it as often as possible. They saw it as beautiful and perfect. They created the Olympic

---

beloved's educator and military trainer."

Games where, as part of this idolization of the physical, the competitors performed without clothes. Their culture was largely focused on worship of beauty.

According to the Jewish tradition, G-d created a beautiful world and we should certainly appreciate all that we have been given. Attractive surroundings and art can uplift the soul. However, for Jews, beauty is not the end goal but a means. We do not worship beauty, but rather appreciate it as a part of our process of moral and spiritual development.

The differences between our view and the Greek view are profound. Worshipping beauty leads to killing deformed babies and the handicapped (something both Greece and Nazi Germany had in common), for they don't fit into an ideal, beautiful world. Worshipping G-d leads to helping others, irrespective of what they look like, and also leads to understanding that true beauty is moral and spiritual, not physical.

Chanukah Bush

Christmas in the Western World is overwhelming. For months, we are surrounded by movies, songs, sales, commercials, advertisements, vacation packages, parties, and more. No wonder that many Jews have placed extra emphasis on Chanukah as a kind of cultural counterweight. Yet for some, Chanukah's role has shifted; instead of it being a buffer against the influence of Christmas, the two have been joined together to give the world oxymoronic creations such as "Chanukah Trees" and "Chanukah Bushes."

> ### I Didn't Know That!
> Where is Chanukah hinted to in the Torah? The twenty-fifth word in Torah is *ohr*, light, an allusion to the first light of Chanukah, which is on the twenty-fifth day of the Hebrew month. Also, the twenty-fifth encampment of the Israelites during their forty-year sojourn in the desert was in a place called Chashmonah, hinting to the Chashmona'im, the family of Maccabees, who led the war and ultimately prevailed on the twenty-fifth day of *Kislev*.

It is crucial that Chanukah not be thought of as the "Jewish Christmas." The Maccabees fought and died for the preservation of Judaism, and not for its combination with Greek beliefs. The very message of Chanukah itself is that we must strive to stay Jewish, and not start down the endless road of assimilation. The very message of Chanukah is that there is no such thing as a "Chanukah Bush."

Jewish Home

Interestingly, we are supposed to light the Menorah with the entire family together. Ideally we light at the front door to the home, the gateway to Jewish family life. Perhaps the reason that Menorahs are supposed to be lit in homes is to teach us that ultimately Jewish continuity depends on the vitality of the Jewish home.

Why Eight Days?

There is a famous question[27] regarding the number of days of Chanukah we celebrate. If the oil that the Maccabees found was sufficient to last one day, and it lasted eight days, then the miracle itself really only lasted seven days. Why, then, is Chanukah celebrated for eight days?

One answer[28] is that the Maccabees knew it would

---

27   Known as the Beit Yosef's question, named after the commentator who asked it.

28   Many other answers exist as to what the "extra miracle" was: (1) The Greeks searched through the entire Temple area for an extended period of time in order to defile all the oil that could possibly be used. They missed one flask, despite their large numbers and unlimited resources. Miraculously, a few exhausted Jews found it immediately (Hameiri, *Lehodot U'lehallel; Sefer HaEshkol, Chanukah* 6:13). (2) Seven days of the holiday commemorate the miracle of the oil and one day commemorates the miracle that a small number of untrained Jewish soldiers beat the mighty Greek army (*Kedushat Levi; Pri Chadash*). (3) Some versions of the account read that there wasn't enough oil to last *even one* day (*Sheiltot Derav Achai Gaon*, quoted in *Siddur Otzar Hatefilot*). (4) Alternatively, there would have been enough oil to last one night in a metal

take eight days to produce more oil, so before they lit the Menorah the first time, they divided what little oil they had into eight equal portions. None should have been able to last the night, and each did, and thus all eight days were a miracle.[29]

Menorah, but because the soldiers were impure, initially they needed to make an earthenware Menorah (earthenware is more resistant to impurity). Since earthenware absorbs more than metal, in this temporary earthenware Menorah, the oil shouldn't have made it even one night (Maharshah on *Chulin* 55). (5) Hoping the oil would last longer, they decided to make the flame as small as possible by paring down the wicks to 1/8 of its normal thickness. The miracle was that the candles burned as brightly as they normally do with a large wick (*Chidushei Harim*). (6) Normally the oil would have been enough for one night, but because Chanukah was on Shabbat, they needed to light the candles earlier than normal — before Shabbat came in — and the oil lasted long enough anyway (*Atzei Zayit*). (7) The Torah hinted that Chanukah should last eight days by placing the section describing the Menorah of the Tabernacle right after the section telling us that Sukkot should last eight days (see Leviticus chap 23)(*Rokeach*). (8) When they poured the oil into the Menorah, the jug didn't actually empty out, but stayed full (*Beit Yosef*). (9) Alternatively, the jug did empty out, but when they returned to the Menorah the next morning, they found that all of the oil was still there, despite having burned all night. (10) Since the Greeks outlawed circumcision, which takes place on the eighth day, we celebrate for eight days commemorating our renewed ability to perform it (*Aruch HaShulchan*). (11) All nature is a miracle, even "normal" oil burning brightly.

29　*Beit Yosef, Orach Chaim* 670.

Another beautiful approach is to focus on Jewish history and survival. Defying all rules of history and logic, the Jewish People passed throughout the millennia intact. The world's oldest People, persecuted like no other, we have survived and had an enormous effect on the world. We are the "eighth" miracle.

Preparation and Practices

Chanukah Gelt: Gift money that is given out during the holiday. The Talmud states that every Jew must light Chanukah lights and that a person with no money should go from door to door until enough is collected for at least one candle each night. Since *tzedakah* (charity) should always be given in the most dignified manner possible, the custom arose to give gifts of money during Chanukah so that the needy will get their candle money through "Chanukah *gelt*." Today we generally give *gelt* to children as a present, adding happiness to the holiday.

Dreidels: These are little spinning tops that have the Hebrew letters *nun gimel heh shin* (which stands for *nes gadol haya sham* – "a great miracle was there") written on the sides. Fittingly, in Israel the last letter is a *peh* (which stands for *poh* – meaning *here*, in Israel), so that it reads "a great miracle was here." The custom of playing dreidel dates back to the times of Chanukah itself: the Greeks targeted the study of Torah, which they correctly understood as the source of our identity and strength. Of course, we understood this as well and so kept studying in secret. When studying Torah in small groups, young people would bring out dreidels and pretend to be playing if the enemy occupiers came by. In our times, children play with dreidels throughout the holiday, sometimes betting candies, nuts, raisins, or even their Chanukah *gelt*. In Yiddish, the following game instructions have developed using the letters as reference: *Nun* for *nisht* (player gets "nothing"), *gimel* for *gantz* (player gets "all"), *heh* for *halb* (player gets "half"), and *shin* for *shtell* (player "puts" into the pot).

Candlelighting: Menorahs are used with olive oil, since that was how the miracle occurred, or alternatively other pure oils or even wax candles.[30] On the first night, we light one candle. Thereafter, another candle is added[31] until the eighth night when all eight

---

30   The famous colored candles that come in the little boxes just barely last long enough to publicize the miracle; if you use them, try sticking them in the freezer so they'll last a little longer. Most Jewish bookstores sell longer colored candles, as well as packets of measured oil portions in disposable cups, to be placed in the candleholders of any standard Menorah.

31   There is ancient disagreement between the School of Hillel and the School of Shammai regarding the order of lighting. The School of Shammai said that eight candles should be lit the first night, with one less each subsequent night. This

are lit. An extra candle, called the *shamash*, is used to light the Chanukah candles.[32] The Chanukah lights[33] themselves may not be used for any purpose aside from being viewed. The Menorah[34] should be lit[35] at nightfall, when they are readily visible by passers-by.

Songs and Food: After the lights have been kindled, Chanukah songs (such as the traditional *Maoz Tzur*) are sung, and many families eat Chanukah foods (usually fried with oil, to remember the miracle) such as jelly donuts and latkes.

Jewish Women: Jewish women deserve much of the credit for defeating the Greeks. Greek forces put the town of Betulia under siege. Strong at first, it

---

corresponds with what actually happened historically — as the oil progressively ran out. The School of Hillel explained that we should start with one and add a candle each subsequent night. This order teaches us that we should be moving in the right direction — upwards!

32   The *shamash* is placed at a different height than the rest, or off to the side, in order to show that it is not one of the Chanukah lights.

33   unlike the *shamash*

34   By placing the Menorah at the left side of the entrance to the home, with the mezuzah on the right (as it always is), we surround ourselves with *mitzvot*.

35   Buyer Beware: Some Menorahs commonly sold today, although physically beautiful, are not "kosher." This is usually because the candles are too close together or not in a straight line.

was weakening and on the verge of surrender. A pious widow named Yehudit (Judith) quietly left the city and, displaying much courage and cunning, managed to assassinate the Greek commander. Her courageous act was a key turning point in the war. The Greeks lost morale and generations of Jews were inspired by her heroism. Two Chanukah customs trace themselves to these events: (1) Because women were instrumental in our salvation, women should not do heavy work as long as the lights are burning; (2) Many people eat cheese during Chanukah in order to commemorate Yehudit's cunning — she gave the Greek commander cheese to bring on thirst and gave him wine to drink. When he fell asleep in a drunken stupor, she killed him.

Asarah BeTevet, literally (the fast of) the tenth (day of the month) of *Tevet*, is a minor fast day commemorating the beginning of the siege of Jerusalem and other[36] tragic events. It lasts from

---

36   What happened on this day? This fast of the Tenth of *Tevet* is really a combination of three separate tragedies. Since it would be too difficult to fast all three days, our sages combined their commemoration into one day, the tenth of the month. The eighth of *Tevet* was the day that the Torah was translated into Greek. Interestingly, when King Ptolemy of Egypt forced seventy Jewish scholars to translate the Torah into Greek, a miracle occurred: though they were each isolated in separate rooms, unable to communicate with each other, they all came up with the same translation. Despite this, and despite the

great advantages of Torah translations in our day, Jewish tradition has viewed this Greek translation as very negative. The Talmud says that when the translation occurred, "darkness descended on the world." Why? Unlike translations today whose goal is to explain and spread Judaism, the goal of the Greek translation — called the Septuagint — was part of a larger attempt to wean Jews away from Hebrew, Judaism, and authentic Jewish life, instead instilling Greek values into the core of our religion and culture.

The ninth of *Tevet* was the day of the death of Ezra the Scribe. Ezra was considered such a great Torah scholar and leader that the Talmud says, "If the Torah had not been given through Moses, it could have been given through Ezra." After the destruction of the First Temple and a seventy-year exile in Babylon, Ezra led us back to Israel and organized the building of the Second Temple. Through Ezra's leadership, Jewish education and observance were greatly strengthened. It is difficult to imagine if or how Jews would have survived without him, and his death was thus rightly considered a great loss for the Jewish People.

The Tenth of *Tevet* was the day that the Assyrian general, Nebuchadnezzar, lay siege to Jerusalem, thus marking the beginning of our eventual defeat, the destruction of the Temple on the Ninth of Av, and our exile.

Fast days are important for every generation to learn from. But these events seem far away — how can we relate to them? How do these "ancient" events affect us today? The three events described here all are rooted in the loss of Torah: the forced Greek translation took us away from authentic Judaism, Ezra's death marked the end of his revitalization of Judaism, and the siege of Jerusalem marked the beginning of the end of Jerusalem inspiring and teaching the Jewish People and the whole world. The Tenth of *Tevet* can therefore

sunrise to sunset and occurs in the winter, shortly after Chanukah.

Chanukah Fast Facts

Name: Chanukah literally means "dedication," for on it we removed the idols installed by the Greeks and rededicated the Temple to the service of G-d.

Summary: We light candles for eight nights to celebrate our victory over the Greeks and the miracle of the oil that lasted for eight days.

Timing: Twenty-fifth of *Kislev*, in the winter, lasting eight nights and days.

help remind us of the centrality of Judaism — the Torah — in our lives and spur us to rededicate ourselves to its study.

Questions for Discussion:[37]

1. Explain what the word Chanukah means.
2. Which parts of Judaism did the Greeks target in particular?
3. The Greeks and Nazis were both great enemies of the Jews. How did they differ?
4. What do the letters on the dreidel stand for?
5. Who was Judith?
6. How do we light the Menorah?

---

37 Most of these questions have numerous answers. Here are a few ideas for easy reference, to help your discussion: (1) Dedication, for we rededicated the Temple. It also refers to "resting" or "finding grace" on the twenty-fifth [of *Kislev*]. (2) Shabbat, circumcision, sanctification of the new moon and Torah study. (3) The Greeks wanted us to become Greek and therefore tried to force their worldview upon us. The Nazis wanted us all dead and therefore tried to kill every last Jewish man, woman, and child. (4) Outside of Israel, the letters are *nun gimel heh shin*, which stand for *nes gadol haya sham* — "a great miracle was there." In Israel, the last letter is a *peh* (which stands for *poh* — meaning "here"), so that it reads, "a great miracle was here." (5) A Jewish heroine who killed the Greek general and inspired the Jews to keep fighting. (6) From left to right

Chapter 6:
Purim

"They are to observe these as days of feasting and gladness, and for sending delicacies to one another, and giving gifts to the poor."

(Esther 9:22)

Purim is a fun-filled holiday in which we commemorate how in Persia, over 2,500 years ago, Esther and Mordechai led our people to salvation from the evil Haman and his accomplices. The name "Purim" literally means [the feast of] "Lots," for Haman drew lots to determine on which day the Jews were to be destroyed. On this enjoyable day, we read the Scroll of Esther (*Megillat Esther* in Hebrew), give charity to the poor, give gifts of food to friends, and have a special Purim meal. Purim lasts one night and one day and occurs in the late winter, one month before Passover.

Purim is a day of community and togetherness; friends visit each other and the poor are welcome everywhere. Yet Purim is anything but calm. The whole of Israel is one big celebration, and in Jewish communities everywhere there is music blaring, people dancing in the streets, and silliness as far as the eye can see.

A Summary[38] of the Purim Story

The events of Purim take place in Persia, approximately 2,500 years ago. At the time, King Ahaseuraus[39] rules the entire civilized world. He holds a huge feast[40] for his subjects in the capital city of Shushan. At the feast, Ahaseuraus asks the evil Queen Vashti[41] to parade without clothing in front of

---

38 No summary can replace the drama, intrigue, beauty, and wisdom of the Megillah itself. Reading it is crucial to celebrating the holiday.

39 His name is pronounced and sometimes spelled Achashverosh; Persia is now known as Iran.

40 The party was essentially a (as it turns out, premature) celebration of his final victory over the Jews, after the destruction of the Temple and failure to return to Israel. He flaunted his disdain for the conquered Jews by wearing the special clothes of the High Priest and by displaying holy vessels stolen from the destroyed Temple in Jerusalem. He invited the Jews to the feast as well, in effect asking them to accept their own downfall. Unfortunately, many Jews attended.

41 The circumstances of Vashti's death are a classic example of how the world works "measure for measure," for she was wicked and had forced Jewish girls to do work on Shabbat, unclothed.

his guests. She refuses.[42] He gets angry and has her killed. The king's servants search for a new queen, and, against her will, the righteous Esther is chosen. She keeps her Jewish identity secret. Providentially, her uncle Mordechai, a great Torah scholar, overhears[43] two guards planning to assassinate the king. He tells Esther, who then tells the king, and the plot fails. Without the king's knowledge, Mordechai's act is recorded in the royal chronicles.[44]

The evil Haman becomes the king's prime minister. Mordechai refuses to bow down to him.[45] Haman is enraged, slanders the Jews to the king as "different" and thus dangerous,[46] and convinces the king to allow

---

42 She had been willing to display herself until she was struck with a terribly embarrassing skin disease.

43 The guards were speaking a rare Persian dialect that they assumed no one could understand. Like all members of the Sanhedrin, the Jewish High Court, Mordechai was required to know seventy languages and therefore understood them.

44 The royal chronicler was an anti-Semite and wanted the act forgotten.

45 Various explanations exist as to his refusal. Here are two examples. First, Haman put an idol around his neck and Jews are forbidden to bow to idols. Second, there was no idol and technically Mordechai could have bowed, but he refused to in an attempt to reawaken the Jewish community to their heritage and religion.

46 His claim is a startling echo of anti-Semitic venom spewed throughout the centuries, "the Jews insist on being different ... let us kill them."

him to get rid of the Jews. A genocidal plan is in place and the life of every Jew is in danger.

One evening, the king cannot sleep[47] and reviews the royal chronicles, for the first time becoming aware that Mordechai saved his life. In appreciation, the king commands Haman[48] to dress Mordechai in royal clothing and lead him around the city on the king's white horse.

Esther commands the Jews to fast and pray.[49] She reveals her identity and begs the king for mercy on her and her people. The king orders Haman to be hanged[50] on the same gallows[51] that he'd prepared

---

47 Angels kept him up in order that he should find out about Mordechai.

48 Haman came to the palace seeking the king's permission to hang Mordechai on the tall gallows he had just built.

49 Throughout history, Jews have held special prayer assemblies and fast days whenever threatened. The Fast of Esther, which occurs the day before Purim, is named after this fast that she commanded, but actually commemorates the fast that Jews always hold before any battle — to remind ourselves that true deliverance comes from spiritual strength, not physical strength.

50 What changed from his happy acquiescence to our destruction? Commentators suggest that Haman represents the active anti-Semites throughout history, who have openly sought to oppress and destroy us. The king represents the silent anti-Semites, who will let things happen and not lift a finger to save us. In this case, the fickle king's feelings for Esther let him switch sides quickly.

51 This is a wonderful example of the *"venahafoch"* (switching)

for Mordechai and then the king allows the Jews to defend themselves against their enemies. Throughout the kingdom, the Jews defeat their enemies on the fourteenth of *Adar*, the day we celebrate Purim.[52]

Mordechai and Esther decree an annual Jewish holiday, with feasting, giving gifts to the poor, food to friends, and reading of the Megillah.

Coincidence

At first glance, the Megillah seems full of coincidences. A king decides to kill his wife. He has a contest to choose her replacement. Esther wins. Esther's uncle Mordechai overhears a plot to kill the king, and saves him. The king's advisor wants to kill the Jews. Before anything happens, the king can't sleep and hears about Mordechai's kindness. The Jews are saved. Individually, any of these events could happen and be labeled a random event, or a mere coincidence.

Purim teaches us to look at the big picture. All these "coincidences" add up to more than chance. The pieces of the puzzle fit together perfectly.

---

theme of Purim, where what Haman planned for Mordechai happened to him, and what our enemies planned for the Jews happened to them.

52   In the capital city of Shushan, the fighting took an extra day, and so there and other ancient walled cities (including Jerusalem today) celebrate on the fifteenth of *Adar*.

Esther just "happened" to be chosen queen and thus be instrumental in our salvation. Mordechai just "happened" to overhear a conversation and save the king's life, thus protecting his own life and those of the Jews of his times. The list of coincidences in the Purim story is amazing. For us, now, it is easy to see G-d's beautiful orchestration of the events — how every piece was carefully put in place for later use. Of course, at the time, it was not so easy to understand what was happening; only hindsight is 20/20.

The lesson of Purim is thus extremely profound: G-d does not openly show His presence in the world.[53] But G-d has not left us to chance, allowing coincidence to run our lives. Behind the scenes, G-d is running the show, deeply involved in our lives.

Jewish Unity

On Purim, it is important to send gifts not just to friends, but especially to people who have just moved into the neighborhood and probably don't know many people yet, and to people we might not be getting along so well with at the moment. We give gifts and charity in order to foster feelings of love and unity within the Jewish People, and in order that Purim should be a time of joy for all, rich and poor alike. The

53   In order to give us free will — the opportunity to *choose* good.

Purim meal is spent with family and friends, and the Megillah is read in shul, also emphasizing the unity of the Jewish community.

Why this emphasis on Jewish unity? Neither the evil Haman nor his modern equivalent, Adolf Hitler, discriminated amongst Jews — we all shared the same fate no matter our differences. Just as in times of trouble we come together, so in this time of joy we should reach out to other Jews, irrespective of any religious, social, or economic differences. The Jewish People is always stronger when we focus on what unites us rather than what separates us.

Yom Kippur and Purim

On Yom Kippur, we wear white clothes, spend the day in shul, fast, repent, and try to rise above the physical, living the day like angels. It is not surprising therefore that Yom Kippur is widely referred to as the holiest day of the Jewish year. On Purim, we dress in funny costumes, spend time with family and friends, eat delicious food and get a little drunk. Great fun, but from a "religious" point of view, it doesn't seem so "holy."

It is somewhat surprising then that Jewish mysticism understands Yom Kippur's Hebrew name, *Yom Hakippurim*, as Yom (a Day) Ki-Purim (*like* Purim).

The implication is that Purim is even greater than Yom Kippur! How can this be?

Our mystical teachings explain that the same spirituality and holiness that we strive for through the "afflictions" of Yom Kippur are available in the "pleasures" of Purim. Yom Kippur is a day of rising above the physical and spending one day living in a purely spiritual world. We ignore our bodies and let our souls connect to G-d. Purim thus has even greater potential. Instead of denying the physical in order to attain spirituality, we can bring the physical along with us. "Mundane pleasures" suddenly attain great meaning and holiness. On Purim, we remind ourselves that meaning and holiness can be attained in the physical world as well.

Flip

The Jews were to be destroyed, yet ended up destroying their enemies. Haman wanted the honor of being led around by Mordechai on the king's horse, yet ended up leading the horse for his enemy Mordechai. The gallows he built for Mordechai were, in the end, used for him. Our enemies wanted to destroy us, yet ended up being destroyed. Purim is the day of "*venahafoch*," in which everything gets "turned upside down" and flipped around. We should never give up hope, for Purim reminds us that things can change, sometimes very quickly.

Don't Worry, Be Happy

Purim also reminds us that G-d wants us to be happy! Sadness and depression don't lead to meaning and spirituality. Happiness can and should lead to fulfillment, direction, meaning, and connection to G-d. As Rabbi Nachman of Breslov put it, "it is a great mitzvah to be happy."

Grandma Sarah's Story

When my wife's grandmother was a little girl in Tel Aviv in the 1920s, there was a neighborhood Arab boy who became friendly with her. One day word went out to stay inside and hidden; Arabs were rioting, killing any Jews they could find. They came to her house, and she heard her young friend tell them, "not here ... they aren't Jewish," saving the family's lives. A listener naturally remarked how nice the boy was, but Grandma Sarah responded harshly, "Nice? You call that nice? He just happened to like me! He went down the street with the others assaulting and murdering innocent people!"

We sometimes make this mistake with the Purim story. We think that Haman was evil, and King

Ahaseuraus saved us by letting us defend ourselves.
But wait a minute! The king was not only willing to
accept a bribe of 10,000 talents of silver to annihilate
the entire Jewish People, but actually said: "The silver
is given to you as well as the people, to do with them
as you see fit."[54] He even gave Haman the royal signet
ring to assure full royal authority for Haman's planned
genocide. In the end, when the fickle king turned
against Haman, it wasn't out of love for the Jews, but
as a result of Esther's courage and wise planning.

Historically, Haman is an example of the active
anti-Semites in our history, openly out to persecute
us. The king is an example of those who prefer to keep
their hands clean but will gladly turn a blind eye and
let genocide occur. Persian Jews were shocked at the
decree of their destruction, much like the German
Jews were about seventy years ago. Yet perhaps the
surprise was not so much at the few radicals yelling
"kill the Jews." Perhaps the surprise was more at the
masses who were willing to let it happen.

The Power of Threats

The Talmud comments[55] that the threat of
destruction hanging over the heads of the Jews

---

54   Esther 3:11
55   Megillah 13a

accomplished more than the exhortations of the fifty-five prophets and prophetesses of the first Temple period. In other words, all their encouragement, warnings, and teachings could not get the Jews of the time to wake up and correct their behavior, while the anti-Semitic sword at our necks quickly caused us to come together and rededicate ourselves to our heritage. The lesson is powerful: just as people should not wait for a heart attack in order to establish proper eating and exercise habits, so too we should not wait for anti-Semitism to remind us that we are Jewish.

I Didn't Know That!

Throughout history, countless nations have targeted the Jewish People for destruction. Some, such as the Nazis, focused on our physical destruction and tried to kill every last Jewish man, woman, and child. Some, such as the Greeks, focused on our spiritual destruction: they would leave us physically alive but without any traces of our Jewish identity. On Chanukah, when we celebrate the victory over the Greeks, who attacked us spiritually, we celebrate spiritually by lighting the Menorah, with no actual mitzvah of feasting. On Purim, since Haman tried to physically destroy us, we celebrate physically with eating, drinking, and merriment.

Preparation and Practices:

Getting Ready: In the days before Purim, families spend the time preparing their festive meals, looking for costumes, and getting their food gifts ready.

Taanit Esther: In ancient times, Jewish soldiers would fast the day before battle in order to remind themselves that true victory came from G-d, not physical prowess. In honor of Esther having saved the entire Jewish People, this minor fast of "The Fast of Esther," occurring on the day before Purim is named for her. It also reminds us of the three-day fast she commanded the entire Jewish People to make before she risked her life and approached the king. This fast does not commemorate a tragedy, but rather helps us focus spiritually before the holiday of Purim.

Half-Shekel: There is an ancient custom to contribute three half-dollar coins[56] to charity shortly before Purim begins.[57] We give a "half" instead of a "whole" in order to symbolically acknowledge that we will never be "whole" without other Jews. There was great disunity among the Jews at the time of the events of Purim. Then, our enemies reminded us that we are one people. Now, the half-shekel donation

---

56 In local currency
57 This symbolizes the half-shekel that every Jew used to give to the Holy Temple in Jerusalem at this time of year.

reminds us of our dependence on each other.

Hearing the *Megillah*: The mitzvah of hearing the *Megillah* is so important that nearly all other commandments are postponed for it. The *Megillah* is read twice — first at night, and again the next day. Special blessings are said before and after the reading. *Megillah* reading is especially enjoyed and looked forward to by children; they bring flags and *graggers* (traditional noisemakers), and stamp[58] their feet every time the evil Haman's name is chanted,[59] thus defeating Haman once again.

***Mishloach Manot* (The Sending of Gifts)**: This mitzvah is fulfilled by sending at least one other person a gift that consists of at least two portions of ready-to-eat food. The food can include anything from cooked meat or fish, to pastries, fruit, sweets, wine, etc, and should be given on the day of Purim itself. The best way to do the mitzvah is to send your gift via a messenger since this gets more people involved in the joy of giving.

***Matanot La'evyonim* (Gifts to the Poor)**: We fulfill this by giving money[60] to at least two poor

---

58   As per the command to wipe out the remembrance of Amalek (Deuteronomy 25:17–19)
59   Though it is important that everyone hear all the words of the Megillah
60   At least enough for an inexpensive meal

people. Each Jewish person should give to the poor, either directly or to a community representative, as long as the money is distributed to the poor on Purim day itself. [61]

Purim Meal: A festive Purim meal is enjoyed on the day of Purim, with family and friends, or at the local synagogue.

Hamantaschen: On Purim, we eat three-cornered cookies called *hamantaschen*. These cookies are cooked dough filled with something tasty beneath the dough, on the inside. One of the main lessons of Purim is to look beyond superficial pretenses and see what is really going on "beneath the surface."[62] In Israel, they are called *oznei Haman*, Haman's ears, because it is said that his ears were triangle-shaped.[63]

---

61 This money is not to be included in what is set aside for charity during the rest of the year. Maimonides states that it is inappropriate to buy expensive gifts for friends if it will limit one's gifts to the poor.

62 Many eat *kreplach* (dumplings) for the same reason.

63 Some explain that the word *Hamantaschen* is a combination of two Yiddish words *mon* (poppy seed) and *tash* (pocket). The translation would therefore be, "a pocket filled with poppy seed" — the food that Esther ate in the king's palace. The prefix *heh* makes it sound like Haman, who we are "consuming." Some families make special cookies with the names of the villainous Vashti and Zeresh on them for the same reason.

Rabbi Yaakov Berlin, father of the famous Netziv, explained

Costumes: Children and many adults wear costumes on Purim. Doing so adds to the fun and joy of this day, but there are deeper reasons as well. Costumes and pretending to be someone else are recurrent themes during Purim. Esther conceals her Jewishness in the royal palace. Mordechai's identity as the king's savior is hidden. G-d hides Himself through the many years that the story unfolds. We therefore dress up, appearing differently than we really are, to remind ourselves that life is not always as it appears.

Purim shpiels: In Europe, villages would enact satirical plays and comedies in keeping with the festive spirit of the day. Even today, many Jewish schools put on Purim plays called *Purim shpiels*, full of skits, songs, and creative jokes. There is a special phrase for the satirical, nonsensical and funny discourses that abound on this day: "Purim Torah."

Drinking: The Talmud tells us that on Purim, one should drink until "one doesn't know between 'Cursed be Haman' and 'Blessed be Mordechai.'" What is the idea of not knowing the difference between these

---

that in our great moment of danger, our three forefathers Abraham, Isaac, and Jacob pleaded with G-d to spare the Jewish People. In their merit, Haman's power weakened. The Hebrew word for "weaken" is *tash*. The three-cornered cookie (one for each forefather) is named *Haman-tash*, "Haman was weakened." (From *Sarei Hameah*)

two phrases? In our normal, sober view of life, we see the victory of the good as representing the greatest manifestation of G-d's justice and compassion in the world. On Purim, when we are slightly intoxicated and outside of our normal frames of reference, we can appreciate that there is another manifestation of G-d's justice and compassion in the world — the downfall of evil. There is really no difference between the blessings of Mordechai and the curse of Haman.

Purim Fast Facts

Name: The name Purim literally means "lots," referring to the lots the evil Haman drew in order to determine which day the Jews were to be destroyed.

Summary: Purim celebrates our victory over those who tried to destroy us in Persia 2,500 years ago. On it, we listen to the Megillah (scroll) of Esther, give money to the poor, give gifts to friends and neighbors, and enjoy a special Purim feast.

Timing: The fourteenth day of *Adar*, in the late winter, one month before Passover.

Questions for Discussion:[64]

1. How is Purim celebrated differently in Jerusalem than in the rest of the world?
2. How many times do we read the Megillah on Purim?
3. What is the name of the noisemaker used on Purim?
4. Name the four main *mitzvot* of Purim.
5. Over how many years do the events of the Purim story span?
6. What are the main lessons of the holiday?

---

64   Many answers exist. Here are a few ideas to get you talking: (1) In most of the world, Purim is celebrated on the fourteenth of Adar. In Jerusalem (and other ancient walled cities) it is celebrated on the fifteenth. (2) Once at night, and once the next morning. (3) *Gragger* (4) Hearing the Megillah, giving to the poor (*matanot la'evyonim*), giving gifts (*mishloach manot*), and eating the festive Purim meal. (5) Ten years (6) Some ideas include: G-d is really behind the scenes, orchestrating events for our benefit even when we don't readily see His hand; things can change quickly; mundane things such as eating and drinking, when done with the right context and with the right perspective, can be uplifting and even holy.

Chapter 7:
Passover

"In every generation, a person is obligated to see himself as if he were leaving Egypt."

(Passover Haggadah)

During the lifetime of the patriarch Jacob, famine forced Jacob's children to relocate to Egypt. Their brother Joseph had already become the leader of the country, second only to Pharaoh. Joseph kept his brothers and their families protected and safe throughout the famine. When a new king arose who did not recognize all the good that Joseph had done for Egypt, the persecution and eventual enslavement of the Jews began. G-d chose Moses as the leader of the Jews. Pharaoh refused to let the Jews leave Egypt. G-d had Moses perform miracles, and struck the Egyptians with plagues in order to force them to "let the Jewish People go." Finally, on G-d's command, Moses led the Jewish People on their Exodus from Egypt, with the help of his siblings, the prophet Aaron and the prophetess Miriam. Passover celebrates the "Exodus" — the leaving — from Egypt.

A joyous holiday, Passover has always been one of the focal points of the Jewish year. Every spring we celebrate this miraculous departure from Egypt on the exact same night that the Israelites left Egypt over 3,000 years ago. The first two nights[65] we enjoy the Passover Seder, one of the most beloved of all Jewish rituals, by reading through the Haggadah in the company of family and friends. We eat matzah (flat, unleavened bread) on this night and throughout the holiday, commemorating our ancestors' quick departure from Egypt when the bread did not even have time to rise. Since we are not allowed to eat anything with *chametz* (leavening) in it, food eaten[66] during the holiday must be supervised to be "Kosher for Passover."

The Names of Passover

The Hebrew name for Passover is Pesach, which literally means "pass over," thus giving us its common English name. The explanation for this strange name is as follows: Time after time, the Egyptians refused to let us leave Egypt no matter what plagues G-d struck them with. The final plague was devastating; all firstborn Egyptian sons were killed. Moses told

---

65   One night in Israel
66   Except for fruits and vegetables

the Jews to slaughter a lamb and put the blood on the doorpost in order to indicate to the angel of death that he should "pass over" the house and not touch the firstborns inside. Passover is also referred to as *Chag Hamatzot*, the Holiday of Matzot; *Zman Cherutainu*, the Time of Our Freedom; and *Chag Heaviv*, the Holiday of Spring. It lasts for eight nights and days and occurs in the early spring.

The Popularity of Passover

Passover is the most popular Jewish holiday of the year. Many Jews attend Seders for family togetherness, enjoyment of the Seder's songs and stories, and nostalgia. However for many, Passover's popularity is even deeper. Passover touches the Jewish heart and the Jewish soul possibly more than any other holiday. Passover is about our common Jewish past and our common Jewish future. It teaches us that we are part of a chain, linking all the way back to the ancient Hebrews who left slavery in Egypt to receive the Torah and to live in Israel. Because Passover represents the link to our history and our heritage, we should make a point on this night to tell each other and ourselves what is really important — where do we come from, how did we survive, and why is it so important that we remain committed to our heritage.

The Message of the Exodus

Dozens of commandments remind us of the Exodus, with some of the most famous ones including *mezuzah*, *tefillin*, and the *Shema*. Countless references are made to the Exodus in Jewish texts. The Exodus is prominent in our prayers and is central to the special Shabbat blessings we say over wine. Why so much emphasis on this one event?

The Exodus is prominent in Jewish life and thought because it reminds us that G-d is active in our lives. The Exodus teaches that not only did G-d create the world, but that He is active in history. The message of the Exodus is repeated over and over because it is in essence the central message of Judaism: G-d is not only all-powerful, but also ever-present, caring about each and every one of us, and always with us.

Freedom for the Ages

Freedom for the Jews? Are you kidding? Since the original Exodus, we've spent more time out of Israel than in it. Our history is full of exiles, pogroms, persecutions, and anti-Semitism, and sometimes overwhelming poverty. More often than not, we have been at the mercy of our neighbors. Even today, it is hard to say that we are really "free" when we consider terrorism, international pressures, boycotts, and anti-

Semitism. Can it be that Passover — a focal point of the Jewish year — celebrates an ancient freedom that no longer exists?

Jamaican music legend Bob Marley had a famous hit album called *Exodus*. Many of the lyrics are clearly based on different chapters of Psalms referring to the Jewish exile in Babylon and the dream of going back to our "Fathers' land in Zion," as the words of the song said. Why did Bob Marley, a dreadlocked Rastafarian, sing about the Jews?

He didn't. He was singing about the Caribbean wish to be freed from colonial bonds. Similar to African slaves and oppressed people everywhere, the Jewish Exodus experience had become a paradigm. We taught the world that things can change. Just because we are oppressed now doesn't mean it will be this way forever. Just because we are enslaved now doesn't mean it will always be this way. We can be free. The Jewish departure from Egypt is the classic vision of the future, a model that gives hope to the downtrodden to look beyond present injustice and envision what can be. It is no wonder that Jews (even highly assimilated ones) have been at the forefront of so many progressive movements; the message that things can become radically better is ingrained in the Jewish consciousness through our history and religion.

The freedom we celebrate on Passover is not simply a commemoration of a piece of history. Passover is the celebration of the possibility and hope of freedom — for the Jews and the entire world.

The Meaning of Matzah

What is the difference between bread and matzah? Bread is allowed to rise fully. When making matzah, we do not allow time for the leavening process to take place and therefore the matzah is not allowed to "rise" into bread.

At a deeper level, leavening (*chametz*) represents the "rising" of the ego — arrogance. Through the search for *chametz* (which includes all leavened products), we remind ourselves of the mistake of arrogance. As we remove *chametz* from our homes, we likewise strive to remove it from ourselves.

Interestingly, Jewish tradition teaches that matzah is really only matzah if the flour used is capable of becoming leavened with no outside intervention; the classic example is wheat flour. Other kinds of flour, such as potato starch, will never become leavened on its own, and therefore can never be matzah.

But why? If we are trying to avoid *chametz* (leavening), wouldn't it be best to use ingredients that could never become *chametz* at all? Why use ingredients that can indeed become leavened, thus forcing us to stop the process before it is too late?

The Chatam Sofer explained that this "legal detail" can teach much about life, and is a principle of Judaism. Avoiding *chametz* in potato starch (where it can never occur) is an irrelevant achievement. The goal is not to *avoid chametz* — that would be easy — the goal is rather to *stop* the *chametz* process. The Talmud[67] teaches a similar lesson: When Moses went up to Heaven to receive the Torah, the angels argued that with all their imperfections and failures, mortals were not worthy of receiving the Torah. Moses answered that angels lack an evil inclination and all the faults that are caused by it (greed, anger, etc). They have no challenges and thus have no need for the Torah, which G-d created to help us struggle with the "evil" part of ourselves.

Matzah is only really matzah when it is made with flour that we have taken control of and not allowed to become *chametz*. Judaism — i.e., the Torah — is for us, not for the angels. Life is only really life when we have "animal" drives that we learn to control and channel into positive outlets.

67   *Shabbat* 88b

Four Questions, More Questions

A most famous and endearing part of the Passover Seders is "The Four Questions," asked by the youngest child, beginning with, "Why is this night different from all other nights?" The goal of many things we do differently on Seder night, such as hiding the *Afikomen*, is to inspire them to ask[68] even more questions. In all of Judaism, in fact, questions are highly valued — sometimes even more than answers — because they are ideal vehicles for growth and change. They get us involved and open us up to new answers and new information. By stimulating children's interest and curiosity, the lessons of the night will be better understood and remembered. By asking the questions, children[69] are really asking why we celebrate Passover

---

68   *Pesachim* 114b

69   It is fitting that children are focused upon in our commemorations, since they were singled out for persecution by the Egyptians. The verses testify to several particular roles of the children: (1) Pharaoh ordered the midwives to kill all male Jewish babies (Exodus 1:16). (2) All male Jewish newborns were to drown in the river (ibid. 1:22). (3) When Pharaoh finally gave in and allowed the Jews to leave Egypt and worship G-d in the desert for three days, he refused to allow the kids to go (ibid. 10:10). Furthermore, our oral traditions add in several more important (and tragic) events of the times: (1) Despite the unavailability of straw, the Jews had to fill their quota of bricks. If they failed to produce enough, children were cemented into the walls in their

and why we are Jews. It is a unique opportunity to tell them how important it is to keep our heritage alive.

Poor Should Recline

In ancient times, the wealthy would recline on their left sides when eating. So, in this holiday of freedom, at certain points in the Seder we are instructed to recline as well. The Talmud goes out of its way to declare that even the poor should recline at the Seder. Why not just say that all Jews should recline? Why focus on the poor?

Wealthy people usually have little problem reclining; their lives are relatively easy and comfortable. Out of worry and hunger, however, the poor rarely get a good night's sleep. It would not be surprising for them to balk at the "freedom" they have, and consider turning it in for the security of servitude. Therefore the Talmud reminds the poor: even you must recline. Your ancestors were slaves in Egypt who were persecuted and beaten. When the right time came, though, G-d punished their oppressors and took them out of Egypt

---

stead. (2) When Pharaoh was struck with leprosy, he ordered the slaughter of Jewish children in order to bathe in their blood. (3) The Egyptians burned many Jewish children in their furnaces. (4) The Egyptians did their utmost to disrupt normal marital life in order to prevent Jewish children from being born.

into their own land. You, therefore, should recline, for no matter how difficult life is for you now, the G-d of Israel has not forgotten you, and your lot can change quickly and dramatically.[70]

Seventh Day of Passover

Interestingly, the Torah itself does not mention any special event happening on the last day of Passover, despite the fact that a very significant miraculous event did occur then. It was on the seventh day that the Sea split to let the Jews pass through, and then crashed down and killed the Egyptians who chased after us. While the splitting of the Sea is well described in the Torah, why doesn't it specify on which day this pivotal event occurred?

The explanation is that our holidays celebrate our salvation, not the downfall of our enemies.[71] All beings are G-d's creations, and so even when the wicked need to be destroyed, it is still no cause for celebration, and so the Torah wants to "downplay" the actual event and focus instead on the message of Redemption.

Passover Contraband

Rabbi Levi Yitzhak of Berditchev was once walking

---

70   Based on the K'tav Sofer, nineteenth century, Hungary.
71   As explained in the *Book of Our Heritage.*

in the street on the day before Passover. He approached a Russian non-Jew on the street and asked him, "Do you have any contraband goods to sell?"

"Yes" replied the non-Jew, "I've brought in many wares, and you can acquire them from me quite cheaply since I paid no duties on them."

Rabbi Levi Yitzhak kept walking until he met a simple Jew in the street. The rabbi asked, "Can I buy some bread from you?" The Jew was shocked.

"What? Bread? It is Passover today — do you think I am so bad a Jew?" He tried again with several Jews on the street who all met him with the same response.

Rabbi Levi Yitzhak looked up into Heaven and said, "Master of the universe! Look down from Your holy abode and see the greatness of the Jewish People. The Russian Czar has a huge army and many policemen whose job it is to prevent smuggling, yet contraband is everywhere to be found. You wrote in Your Torah,

> ### I Didn't Know That!
> The word "*Soof*" means "reeds". When the Torah says that the Jews crossed the "*Yam Soof*," it literally means that they crossed the "Sea of Reeds," not the Red Sea as it is often translated. Many suggestions exist as to what the *Yam Soof* exactly was, including what is presently called the Red Sea, the Gulf of Suez, and the northern part of the Nile Delta.*
>
> * It is said that the word for "delta" in ancient Egyptian is *sufi*.

'*And there shall be no leaven seen with you in all your borders seven days,*'[72] and the day before Passover 3,000 years later, not a bit of bread can be found! What a People!"

Preparation

***Maot Chittin*:** One of the hallmarks of Jewish communities everywhere is the existence of a charity fund. Throughout our entire history, Jews have made every effort to feed their poor brethren. With the approach of Passover, a special campaign is organized called *Maot Chittin* (money for wheat) or *Kimcha d'Pischa* (flour for Passover) to collect and distribute Passover foods for the needy in every Jewish community.

Getting Rid of *Chametz*: Flour that has been exposed to water within the first eighteen minutes of baking rises and becomes *chametz*, "leavened." On Passover we are careful to avoid eating any leavened product. Common products, such as bread, pasta, non-Passover cookies and cakes, beer, spirits, and many processed foods have *chametz* and are therefore not to be eaten or owned during the holiday.

Cleaning and Searching for *Chametz*: In the

---

72   Deuteronomy 16:4

weeks preceding Passover, any place where *chametz* may have entered is checked and cleaned. On the night before Passover, a search[73] is done around the house. In a ritual[74] that children look forward to, ten pieces of bread are hidden and then found by another member of the family.

Selling *Chametz*: Aside from the prohibition of eating *chametz*, we are not supposed to even *own* any during the holiday. Jewish practice is therefore to sell[75] any *chametz* that we may have forgotten to a non-Jew for the duration of the holiday.

***Kitniyot*:** This is the Hebrew word for legumes, such as peas, beans, and peanuts, and cereals such as rice and corn. While legumes and similar foods are not *chametz*, Ashkenazi custom is not to eat them.[76] Most Sephardic Jews never adopted this custom and

---

73 Customarily with a candle and a feather

74 This is not a token search, rather a real search which helps us find any *chametz* we may have missed. It is recommended to keep a list of where you put the little pieces, because they all need to be found!

75 It is a complicated sale and must be done through a competent expert in Jewish law.

76 Since cakes and breads can be made from both legumes and prohibited grains, we fear that one may come to eat the wrong kind. Also, since legumes and grains are often stored together, they may inadvertently get mixed up and mistakenly consumed.

therefore eat *kitniyot*.[77]

Gebrochts: Yiddish word for "broken." According to Jewish Law, once matzah is baked, it can't become *chametz* again even if it comes into contact with water. Some people are extra-careful and don't eat any matzah that has come into contact with water.[78] They do not eat *gebrochts*, or broken-up matzah. Many other Jews do eat products made with matzah meal, etc., meaning that they eat *gebrochts*.

Fast of Firstborn: The morning before Passover, firstborn males fast in order to recall the miracle of having been saved from the plague of the firstborn. If they attend a happy religious event such as a *siyum*, a completion of a tractate of Talmud, participants are exempt from the fast and allowed to eat.

Seder Night Practices

Passover Seder: The sages of the Talmud set up an order (*seder*) of ceremonies. The word *Seder* has become the popular name for the Passover feast. It includes many components such as the Four

---

77   Although they check carefully to make sure there's no wheat mixed in. Some Sephardic Jews refrain from rice for the reasons above, but eat other types of *kitniyot*.

78   Fearing that perhaps a little pocket of dry flour hidden inside will have become *chametz*.

Questions, the four cups of wine, and the telling of the plagues. The text we use is called the *Haggadah*, meaning the "telling," as the main commandment of the evening (along with eating matzah) is to tell the story of the Exodus from Egypt. The *Haggadah* is an educational and inspirational masterpiece that speaks to all levels of knowledge and interest. Wonderful songs are sung and traditional foods are eaten.

Reclining: In ancient times, the wealthy and free would recline on their left sides when they ate. In each generation, we are to regard ourselves as if we personally were freed from Egyptian bondage, so we recline at different points during the Seder in the manner of free people and royalty.

Maror: We eat bitter herbs such as horseradish to remember the bitterness of the Egyptian exile.

Matzot: Three matzot are placed on the table, representing the three categories of Jews (Kohanim, Levi'im and Israelim) for without true Jewish unity, our future redemption cannot occur.

Afikomen: At the Seder, one of the matzahs is broken and half is hidden away during the meal. Children love trying to find the matzah and then holding it ransom, because the adults need to eat it to finish the Seder and are usually willing to reward the kids for its safe return!

Egg and Roasted Meat are used to symbolize the

Pesach offering. An egg is unique in that as it is boiled, it becomes harder, not softer, like other foods. This represents the Jewish People, who became stronger and stronger the more they suffered.

The Four Questions: The youngest child at the Seder, and in some families all the children, ask "The Four Questions," which are printed in the *Haggadah*. Emotionally, the questions are very important; many fond Jewish memories have been made on Seder night, and especially in the asking of the questions. Educationally, the questions ask why Passover night is different, why *we* are different, and what it means to be Jewish. Much of the rest of the *Haggadah* forms the basis for answering these questions.

Four Cups of Wine: During the Seder, we drink four cups of wine referring to the four different stages of redemption we passed through.

The Song of Songs: One of the books of the Hebrew Bible, the Song of Songs is essentially a love poem between G-d and the Jewish People, and it is thus fitting to read it during the holiday since Passover reverberates with that love.

Elijah's Cup: Tradition explains that the prophet Elijah will announce the coming of the Messiah and the Redemption of the world. Since it is quite fitting that Elijah should arrive at Seder time, when we were redeemed from Egypt, we therefore open the door to allow him to enter easily and to signify that "All who are hungry should come and eat."

In the days and weeks *following* Passover, several unique days occur:

Maimuna: Maimuna is a wonderful North-African Jewish celebration of friendship and feasting on the evening and day following the end of Passover.[79] **Lag B'Omer:** Almost 2,000 years ago, 24,000 students of the great Rabbi Akiva were killed in a plague.[80] *Lag* is

---

79   I've come across many explanations of the celebration and its name: (1) It is the *yahrtzeit* (anniversary of the death) of Rabbi Moses ben Maimon, Maimonides, who lived in the Moroccan city of Fez where this custom originated. (2) The word *mamon* means money. The holiday celebrates the wealth and luxury with which we left Egypt after generations of slavery, and indeed it is customary to bring out gold and silver on this happy day. (3) Moroccan Jews were especially careful during Passover about forbidden foods and individual families had their own traditions about what they did or did not eat. Since different customs made it somewhat difficult to eat at each other's homes during Passover, immediately following the holiday, friends visited each other to emphasize that their "separation" was not personal but a question of family traditions. The first two explanations are discussed in many places, while the last I heard from Rabbi Dovid Tourgeman of Jerusalem.

80   We observe certain mourning practices (i.e., no weddings or haircuts) to mark the loss and hopefully help us to learn from it.

a combination of the letters *lamed* and *gimel*, whose numerical values are thirty and three, respectively. On the thirty-third day of the Omer, the plague stopped. In addition, Rabbi Shimon bar Yochai, author of Judaism's primary mystical work, the *Zohar*, taught the central messages of Jewish mysticism before his own death on this day, and tradition says that a wonderful light filled the world, reflecting the light of the great wisdom he taught his students. Lag B'Omer is thus a day of celebration with dancing, bonfires, and much singing and joy. Hundreds of thousands flock to the mystical Mount Meron near his gravesite in northern Israel. Jewish communities around the world also hold celebrations on this day.

Other Commemorations and Celebrations

Between Passover and Shavuot, the State of Israel has added several unique days to the Jewish calendar: Holocaust Day, Jerusalem Day, Memorial Day, and Israeli Independence Day. Seeing as these days are not classic "religious holidays" per se, I haven't included them here but interested readers should consult our recommended reading lists for more information.

Passover Fast Facts

Name: Pesach literally means "Pass Over" because G-d "passed over" our homes when striking the Egyptians. Passover is also referred to as *Chag Hamatzot*, the Holiday of Matzot, and *Zman Cherutainu*, the Time of Our Freedom.

Summary: We celebrate the Exodus from Egypt with Seders on the first two nights of the holiday, and the eating of matzah instead of *chametz* (leavened products) for the entire holiday.

Timing: Fifteenth of *Nissan*, in the spring, lasting eight nights and days.

Questions for Discussion:[81]

1. What does the name Passover refer to?
2. Why do we eat matzah on Passover?
3. Why is the Passover Seder called a "Seder"?
4. Why do we recline at various stages of the Seder?
5. What is the *Afikomen*?
6. Why do you feel Passover is such a popular holiday?

---

81 Most of these questions have numerous answers. Here are a few ideas for easy reference, to help your discussion: (1) That G-d passed over our homes when he struck the Egyptians. (2) To remind us that they didn't have time to let their bread rise when they left Egypt, and to remind us to be humble rather than "puffed up" and arrogant. (3) It refers to the "order" of ceremonies that we do this evening. (4) To be like free people (5) The last piece of matzah, hidden by the children, and saved for the end of the Seder (6) What do you think?

Chapter 8:
Shavuot

"The Torah is a tree of life to those who hold onto it, and those who support it find happiness."

(Proverbs 3:18)

Shavuot was the day that the Torah was given, and on it we thank G-d for giving us our religion and stay up all night studying its teachings. By reminding us of the giving of the Torah, Shavuot reminds us that each of us is a link in a 3,000-year-old chain, and that we are responsible for passing our heritage on to the next generation.

The word Shavuot[82] literally means "weeks," relating to the seven weeks we count from Passover[83] to Shavuot. The holiday is also called *Zman Matan Torateinu*, the Time of the Giving of our Torah; *Chag*

---

82 Others explain (*Ta'amei Haminhagim* and *Tur Barekes*) that the holiday is called "Shavuot" because of its alternate translation, "oaths." When we accepted the Torah, G-d "swore" not to "exchange" us for any other nation, and we promised that we would not "exchange" G-d for anyone or anything else. The holiday would then be pronounced Shevuot.

83 Beginning with the second day, as per the Torah's instructions.

Hakatzir, the Festival of the Harvest; and *Chag Habikkurim*, the Festival of the First Fruits (for an offering of the first fruits was brought in thanks and celebration of the harvest). Shavuot occurs on the sixth day of the month of *Sivan*, in the early summer.

Oral-Companion Law

Since written words are easily misunderstood and taken out of context, many different religions with different beliefs can base themselves on the same written text. For example, although many groups believe the Five Books of Moses (the Torah) to be Divine, they have ended up with radically different views of life and religion. With no system establishing *how* to understand written words, text is essentially free for all to interpret as they like. One can "stick into" the verses just about any ideas one wants to promote. Religion thus becomes a servant to man's priorities, rather than a Divine guidebook establishing G-d's priorities.

The Giver of the Torah, G-d, was fully aware of this problem and therefore gave us principles and oral[84] traditions (passed down from generation to

---

84   When these traditions and principles were in danger of being lost due to Roman persecutions, they were eventually written down in the Talmud and other works of that era.

generation) along with the written word, providing a system for understanding the written Torah. These oral companions to the Written Word are known as the Oral Law, or the Oral Torah.

The Written Torah itself gives many indications as to the existence of the Oral Torah. One famous example occurs in Deuteronomy 12:21. The Torah says that we need to slaughter our cattle and small animals "in the manner that I have commanded you," *ka'asher tziviticha*, but nowhere in the Torah (or Writings or Prophets, for that matter) is a method of slaughter outlined. It is clear that there must have existed an oral teaching passed down from teacher to student as to what kosher slaughter (*shechitah*) was. Another example concerns *Tefillin*, the little black boxes that are worn on the upper arm and head. The Torah only says that the teachings being discussed should be "a sign on your hand and an emblem on the center of your head" (Deuteronomy 6:8). The commandment of *Tefillin* also occurs in Deuteronomy 11:18, Exodus 13:9, and Exodus 13:16, yet nowhere is any information given as to what they are or how they should be made. Here too, teachers orally taught students how to make *Tefillin* and when and how to wear them.

There are many other examples, but the common denominator is that the Written Torah was never meant to be understood — and cannot be understood

— without the oral traditions surrounding it. The Written Torah is akin to class notes,[85] with the Oral Torah being the full, detailed understanding of the lesson. At Sinai, both the Written and Oral Torahs were given to the Jewish People, in order to preserve accuracy in the understanding of the Torah and thus establish clear boundaries and guidelines for the perpetuation of Judaism.

With this background, we can now understand a perplexing element of Shavuot. Why does the Written Torah itself omit to mention that Shavuot celebrates the giving of the Torah, when the events commemorated by Passover (the Exodus from Egypt) and Sukkot (the protection of the booths in the desert)[86] are clearly

---

85   Based on Rabbi Samson Raphael Hirsch

86   Verses in the Torah state clearly that Passover commemorates the leaving of Egypt and that Sukkot commemorates our journeys in the desert. One would think that Shavuot would thus be openly associated with the giving of the Torah, yet nowhere does the Torah mention this connection. It is left to our oral traditions to fill in this important gap. Many have thus asked, why don't the verses tell us clearly that Shavuot was the day that the Torah was given? The *Aruch Hashulchan* and Rabbi Samson Raphael Hirsch both answer this question in similar ways. Since we left Egypt on a specific day, we thus commemorate it on a specific day. Our time in the desert was a temporary occurrence with a set beginning and end, and we therefore have a set time to commemorate it. Things are different when it comes to the Torah. It — Judaism — is to

outlined? The explanation is that G-d didn't want the Written Law to tell us that the Torah was given on Shavuot because we might think that *only* the written text was given by G-d. Rather, by relying on the Oral Torah to teach us that Shavuot is the holiday of the giving of the Torah, we learn that much more than the written word was given on Shavuot. Oral traditions, principles, and explanations were given as well, thus enabling Judaism to survive intact throughout the generations.[87]

---

permeate our entire lives and affect our thoughts and actions. We study it, yearn for it, laugh with it, and cry with it. So although we do relive the Sinai experience yearly on Shavuot, not having the exact day mentioned reminds us that Judaism does not have a specific day for its commemoration, for our entire lives should be centered around it. In the same vein, the *Chiddushei Harim* remarks that in our prayers, Shavuot is called the Time of the Giving of the Torah, and not *Z'man Kabalat HaTorah* — the Time of the Receiving of the Torah. When our sages wrote the prayers, they wanted to emphasize the fact that while the giving of the Torah occurred only once (and therefore can be celebrated), the receiving of the Torah is an ongoing event occurring in all of our lives regularly, and thus cannot be celebrated on a given day.

87   Similar to this is the reading of the *Book of Ruth* on Shavuot. Although the verse states that "*a Moabite may not marry into the Congregation of G-d*" (Deuteronomy 23:4), Ruth the Moabite was allowed to marry Boaz based on a teaching of the Oral Tradition that explained that the prohibition applied only to the men of the people of Moab. Reading the

Ritual-less Holiday

Passover has matzot. Sukkot has *Sukkot* and the Four Species. Rosh Hashanah has the *Shofar*. Although we customarily eat dairy foods on Shavuot, the holiday is markedly absent of any ritual objects.

> **I Didn't Know That!**
> Why wasn't the Torah given to the Jews in Israel? Our tradition explains that the Torah was specifically not given in the Land of Israel to teach us that it was given for the benefit of the whole world, not just the Jewish People. And why was the Torah given in a desert? To teach us that just as the desert is empty, one needs to be "empty" of pride and arrogance in order to properly receive the Torah and grow spiritually.

Why? Because this is not a day of "doing," at all. The holiday is called *Atzeret* because on it, we simply "stop" for a moment and try to appreciate our amazing religion.[88]

---

story of Ruth at this time thus hints at the unity between the Written Torah and the Oral Torah, and reminds us that they are inseparable. Our dependence on the Oral Tradition is so great that Ruth's descendant David, the king of Israel and ancestor of the Messiah, was only considered Jewish based on the teachings of the Oral Torah.

88 Nachmanides and others point out that this *Chag Ha'atzeret* (Shavuot) "completes" or "ends" Passover just as *Shemini Atzeret* "completes" or "ends" Sukkot.

Receive Torah with Unity

In describing the giving of the Torah, the verse states (Exodus 19:2) that the Jewish People "encamped before the mountain," and strangely uses the singular verb form despite the fact that many people were there. The Torah is telling us that when they encamped at the bottom of Mount Sinai, they were like one person with a single heart. In fact, it had to be this way, for it is only possible to fully receive the Torah when the Jewish People are united.

Preparation and Practices[89]

Greenery: In the days before the holiday, we bring flowers and greenery into our homes and synagogues[90] in order to remember that the Torah was given on a lush mountain ... in the middle of a desert!

Staying Up Late: There is an ancient custom to stay up the entire night studying Torah in anticipation of re-receiving it. Our forefathers slept throughout the night and needed to be woken by G-d in order to

89   Also note that in morning prayers on this day, Ashkenazic Jews recite a 1,000-year-old poem called "Akdamut," which gives a vivid picture of the day that the Messiah will arrive, and portrays our love for and loyalty to G-d despite many challenges.

90   Because of the harvest aspect of the day

receive the Torah. We "fix" this mistake by staying up all night learning in preparation of receiving it once again.[91] There is also a special mystical prayer service, *Tikun Leil Shavuot*, that is studied and recited on the first night of Shavuot. The *Tikun* was organized centuries ago and is a compilation of parts of both the Written and the Oral Torah. One of its noticeable features is that it includes the beginnings and ends of each book in the Written Torah and each of the six books of the Mishnah. By the end of the night, it is as if we had learned the entire Torah.[92]

Eating Milk on Shavuot:[93] Jewish tradition is to

---

91   Rama

92   Sefer *Minhagei Yisrael Torah*

93   Other Shavuot foods: Shavuot has several beautiful culinary customs. Some bake two long challahs to commemorate the two special loaves brought in the Temple on this day of the "First Fruits." Many eat triangle-shaped latkes or *kreplach*, for as it is said, G-d gave a three-part Torah (the Five Books, the Prophets, and the Writings) to a three-part nation (Kohanim, Leviim, Israelim) through a third-born (Moses, after Aron, and Miriam) in the third month (*Sivan*, after *Nissan* and *Iyar*). My favorites have always been the desserts, of course. Cakes are baked or fried in honey, connected to the verse in the Song of Songs (4:11) that states "Milk and honey are under your tongue," referring to the Torah. Friends of ours continue the age-old tradition of making Mount Sinai cakes (traditionally made with honey) with a modern twist: a huge homemade ice-cream cake, shaped like a mountain, with two Popsicle tablets at the top and little M&Ms-people below. In

eat a dairy meal[94] sometime during Shavuot.[95] Many reasons[96] are given for this custom. One historical explanation[97] is that until the Torah gave its kosher food laws, Jews were allowed to eat any meat by any

---

its ancient or modern version, this custom also fulfills a verse, "Taste and see that G-d is good" (Psalms 34:9). Similarly, some introduce children to the Hebrew alphabet on Shavuot, placing honey on top of the Hebrew letters and letting the children lick them off, thus learning that the Torah is sweet.

94   For example, blintzes.

95   Properly separated from the eating of meat, of course

96   Rabbi Shimshon of Ostropol mentions that the numerical value of the Hebrew letters of *chalav*, milk, add up to forty. This corresponds to the forty days Moses spent on Mount Sinai receiving the Torah. The *Sefer Matamim* explains that Moses was drawn out of the water on the day of Shavuot, and he refused to be nursed by anyone but Jewish women, and so our "milk" commemorates his "milk." The Rama emphasizes that Shavuot is really the conclusion of Passover (connected by the Omer). Then, we eat two cooked dishes to commemorate the *Paschal Lamb* and the *Chaggigah* offering, and on Shavuot we also eat two cooked foods — one meat and one milk. It has also been suggested that before Sinai, the Jews were afraid to eat meat out of fear of transgressing the prohibition of eating a limb taken from a living animal, which is prohibited to all of humanity as one of the seven Noachide commandments. As they subsisted on dairy, so do we. Finally, one of the five names for Mount Sinai mentioned in our sources is *gavnonim*, which literally means "free from blemish," but whose Hebrew form indicates a dairy product. (The Hebrew for cheese is *gevinah*.)

97   *Ge'ulat Israel* and the *Mishnah Berurah*.

method of slaughter. Once the Torah was given, meat vessels needed to be made kosher. This took a few days and, in the meantime, they had to eat non-meat foods, i.e., milk. On a symbolic level, it has been suggested that milk symbolizes the infancy of the Jewish People, and their birth as a nation at Mount Sinai.

The Ten Commandments: The Torah reading of the day[98] includes the Ten Commandments, for as well as forming the basic categories of all the commandments,[99] they form the basis for all world morality. Wherever the Ten Commandments went, there is little or no idol worship today. Wherever they did not reach, idolatry in some form exists to this day.

The Ten Commandments are:

1. I am the Lord, Your G-d Who brought you out of Egypt.
2. You shall have no other gods but Me.
3. You shall not take the Name of G-d in vain.
4. Remember the Sabbath day to keep it holy.
5. Honor your father and mother.

---

98   In ancient times, the Ten Commandments were recited as part of the regular daily synagogue service. They were removed from daily prayers because the early Christians claimed that only the Ten Commandments were still true. The Rabbis felt we had to re-emphasize the authority of the entire Torah by ceasing to "focus" on the Ten Commandments.

99   as Rav Saadia Gaon explained

6. You shall not murder.
7. You shall not commit adultery.
8. You shall not steal.
9. You shall not bear false witness against your neighbor.
10. You shall not covet (desire) anything that belongs to another.

Book of Ruth: On Shavuot, we read the *Book of Ruth*, which tells the story of the prophetess Ruth, who leaves behind her country, religion, and family to join the Jewish People. She has been the paradigm of sincere conversion for over 3,000 years, and her famous words have inspired generations: *"Where you go, I will go, and where you stay, I will stay. Your People will be my People, and your G-d my G-d."*[100] There are many reasons[101] why we read the *Book of Ruth* on Shavuot.

---

100 Ruth 1:16

101 Since Ruth did great acts of *chesed* (kindness) throughout her life, we read about her at the very time we receive the Torah, to remind us that you can't really acquire the Torah without caring for other people. The name "Ruth" has the numerical value of 606. At Mount Sinai, we accepted 606 new commandments in addition to the seven Noachide laws that are incumbent upon all human beings (*Teshuos Chen*), thus totaling the famous 613 commandments of Judaism. In other words, her very name hints at her amazing choice of committing to the Torah. The Vilna Gaon explains that this indicates that from her birth, Ruth was worthy of conversion,

On a simple level,[102] the events of her conversion to Judaism occurred during the harvest season of Shavuot, and Ruth's great-grandson, King David, was born and died on Shavuot.[103] On a symbolic level, Ruth was a convert to Judaism. When we accepted the Torah, we were all converts, and as we "accept the Torah" again yearly on Shavuot, we read about her journey to remind ourselves that we should recommit ourselves with as much energy and enthusiasm as a new convert.[104]

Shavuot Fast Facts

Name: Shavuot literally means "weeks," referring to the seven weeks counted since Passover in anticipation of the giving of the Torah on Shavuot.

Summary: We celebrate the giving of the Torah by staying up late to study its teachings and eat dairy foods to remind ourselves how sweet Judaism is.

Timing: Sixth day of *Sivan*, in the early summer, and lasts for two days.

---

for her very name reflects her destiny.

102 *Abudraham*

103 *Taamei Haminhagim*

104 To teach us that just as Ruth's path to receiving the Torah was full of affliction and poverty, so too our receiving the Torah goes through difficulty and pain. To truly "acquire" the Torah, there must be a willingness to sacrifice for it (*Magen Avraham* 490:8).

Questions for Discussion:[105]

1. What does the name of the holiday refer to?
2. What is the connection between Passover and Shavuot?
3. Why do we read the *Book of Ruth* on Shavuot?
4. Why is Shavuot called the Holiday of the Giving of the Torah rather than the Holiday of the Receiving of the Torah?
5. Why was the Torah given in the desert?
6. What was given on Shavuot?

---

105 Many answers can be offered to these questions. Here are a few ideas to help your discussion. (1) "Shavuot" literally means weeks, referring to the counting of the seven weeks between Passover and Shavuot. (2) Passover celebrates our freedom and exodus from the slavery of Egypt. The raison d'etre of the Passover Exodus itself was not simply to survive physically, but in order to receive the Torah on Shavuot. (3) The *Book of Ruth* is read on Shavuot because on Shavuot we all rededicate ourselves to the Torah, just as she did. (4) Shavuot is called the Holiday of the Giving of the Torah rather than the Holiday of the Receiving of the Torah because although it was given once, in the past, it can be received by all of us each and every day. (5) The Torah was given in the desert, which is empty, to teach us that people who are "full" of themselves cannot properly accept or fulfill it. (6) On Shavuot, we were given not just the text of the Torah but also the oral traditions and understandings that make it understandable and consistent throughout the ages.

Chapter 9:
Ninth of Av

By the rivers of Babylon, we sat and wept when we remembered Zion.

(Psalms 137:1)

Tisha B'Av, literally the ninth day of the month of Av, occurs in the summer and is the saddest day of the Jewish calendar. It is a night and day of fasting and prayer in mourning over the destruction of the Holy Temple and other tragedies that occurred on this fateful day. Here is a partial list of events that occurred on the Ninth of Av:[106]

1312 BCE: The Jews believed slanderous reports about the Land of Israel and didn't trust G-d's promise to take care of them. On the ninth of Av, it was therefore decreed that they would need to wander in the desert for forty more years before they could enter Israel.

586 BCE and 70 CE: The First and Second Temples in Jerusalem were destroyed on this same day

---

106 Partially based on a list appearing on ohr.edu. More are listed there and elsewhere.

of the calendar. In the first destruction, over 100,000 Jews were killed and millions were exiled. In the second destruction, over 2 million Jews were killed and millions exiled. Furthermore, over 100,000 were sold into slavery.

133 CE: The Temple area in Jerusalem was plowed over by the Romans on this day, the entire city was quickly stripped of its Jewish identity, and Jews were denied access to their holiest site. The Romans built the city of Aelia Capitolina, full of paganism and hedonism, on its ruins.

135 CE: When Roman oppression became unbearable, the Jews attempted a revolt. Although initially successful, the revolt ended in terrible tragedy. The city of Beitar was captured by Roman emperor Hadrian on this day. Over 100,000 Jews were brutally slaughtered. We would not return to Israel in large numbers for almost 2,000 years.

1095 CE: Pope Urban II declared the First Crusade on this day. In the first month alone, over 10,000 Jews were murdered as the Crusaders rampaged through Jewish communities in Europe. Hundreds of Jewish communities were destroyed and countless numbers murdered and raped along the way.

1290 CE: Jews were forced out of England on this day. Widespread pogroms and theft of property occurred.

1492 CE: The Expulsion from Spain and Portugal occurred on this day, the culmination of the brutal Spanish Inquisition. Many were tortured, hundreds of thousands fled under terrible conditions and hundreds of thousands died of drowning, hunger, and disease.

1914 CE: Russia and Britain declared war on Germany on this day, and during the war over 120,000 Jews were killed. There were countless Jewish communities destroyed and the Jewish social structure was broken down so radically and violently that it never managed to rebuild itself. There were over 400 pogroms across Europe following the war, and German resentment set the stage for the next World War.

1942 CE: Deportation of the Jews of the Warsaw ghetto to Treblinka's death camps began on this day.

1989 CE: On this day, Iraq walked out of talks with Kuwait, precipitating the Gulf War in which millions of Israelis lived in sealed rooms as Scud missiles landed around the country.

1994 CE: The Jewish Community Center in Buenos Aires, Argentina, was bombed on this day, leaving eighty-six dead and hundreds wounded.

This is just a sample of the incredible "coincidence" of tragedies that occurred on this day. It is indeed the saddest day of the year.

Jerusalem

At the end of the Passover Seder, we say, "Next year in Jerusalem!" In our prayers, we constantly ask that Jerusalem be rebuilt. Synagogues around the world are designed to face Jerusalem. At Jewish weddings — our happiest moments — we break a glass in order to remind ourselves of the destruction of Jerusalem. The "Grace after Meals" focuses on Jerusalem and Israel. Sages and scholars have gone to great lengths throughout the ages to simply see the remains of the Temple, and on Tisha B'Av, despite all the tragedies listed above (and many others that weren't listed), still the overwhelming focus of the day is on the loss of the Temple and Jerusalem. Why? What is so special about Jerusalem? Our tradition teaches that Jerusalem is the center of the world, as many medieval maps place it. And the center of Jerusalem is the Temple Mount area. It is where Adam was created from the earth, where Abraham bound Isaac on the altar, where David moved the Tabernacle, and where Solomon built the First Temple.

The Temple was not simply a place to pray, although it served that function as well. The Temple resulted from G-d's desire for a permanent location in the world, an address for His "Presence." Miracles regularly occurred in the Temple, the Divine presence was felt there more than any other place on earth, and visitors left transformed.

Additionally, the Temple did not just affect those who were able to visit it. The site of the Temple is called Mount Moriah because it is from there that "teaching (*hora'ah*) goes forth; from which awe of heaven (*yirah*) goes forth; and from which light (*orah*) goes forth." All three words — teaching, awe, and light — share the same root as Moriah.[107] The Temple was not only a repository of spirituality but a conduit for it as well — even for those who weren't able to enter its precincts.

Furthermore, the Temple was not just of benefit to the Jews. All the blessings of the world flowed through it. The Talmud says that if the Romans had understood how much the Temple helped them, they would have protected it rather than destroyed it.

In essence, we focus on the loss of the Temple because it was a structure like no other. It was G-d's home and the main conduit of goodness and spirituality in the world. Its destruction has left us spiritual orphans.

Why Cry?

Imagine a free man who becomes enslaved. After some time, he adjusts to his new surroundings, forgets

107 Based on Rashi

that he was ever free, or even what freedom was like. He becomes numb and sometimes forgets he is missing anything. He doesn't realize what life should really be like.

The parallel for us is profound: It has been so long that we have survived without a Temple that we no longer sense that we are really missing anything at all.

The story is told of a young peasant boy who heard crying from the local shul, a place he had rarely visited. Entering quietly, he noticed the old men and scholars sitting on the ground sadly, with pools of tears at their feet. The boy began to sob uncontrollably until one old man came up to him and said, "I know why I am crying, but my child, you don't even know what day it is. Why are you crying?" The boy burst out in tears once again and explained, "I'm crying because I don't know why I should be crying."

Without the Temple, connecting to G-d is more difficult. We are "spiritual cripples," not even realizing that we are crippled. Focusing on the Temple on the ninth of Av helps remind us that our lives are not full and complete. Our lives could, and should, be so much more meaningful.

What if you don't feel sad on Tisha B'Av? This is not uncommon. It is not easy for us, so far removed from the tragedy, to actually feel it. Our sages knew this would happen, and the customs of the day are engineered to help us feel the loss.

In fact, all of Jewish practice is both descriptive and prescriptive. For a person who understands and deeply connects to spirituality, the "rituals" he is performing simply reflect or describe his internal reality. For people who do not connect so easily, the "rituals" they are performing help them feel.

On Tisha B'Av, ideally, we should feel the sense of loss so greatly that the mourning practices we engage simply "describe" and reflect our inner reality. But it is not always easy. When we don't feel the sense of loss, the practices are "prescriptive," indicating to us what to do in order to get closer to the appropriate feelings of the day.

Senseless Hatred

Why was the Temple destroyed? On a practical level, the Romans destroyed it. But on a deeper level, why did G-d let it be destroyed?

The Talmud tells us of a certain host of a party who had a friend called Kamtzah and an enemy called Bar Kamtzah. By accident, the enemy got invited instead of the friend.

When the host saw his enemy at the affair, he screamed at him, "Leave at once!"

Bar Kamtzah the enemy replied, "Please don't

embarrass me in front of all these people. Let me stay. I'll even pay for my meal."

"No!" answered the host. "Get out!"

"I'll pay for half the party — just don't throw me out."

"No. Get out immediately."

"I'll pay for the whole party affair!"

The host refused and threw out his enemy, causing him great embarrassment. Bar Kamtzah was so upset at what happened — and that no one interceded to stop the scene — that he began to hate the Jewish community, and went to Rome in order to convince the Caesar that the Jews were rebelling. This complaint ultimately led to the destruction of the Temple. The Talmud thus explains that it was *sinat chinam*, baseless hatred, that caused the destruction of the Temple.

The Jewish People is one big family. We are supposed to treat each other with respect and sensitivity, even when we disagree. When we treat each other properly, we model the ideal society. When we treat each other with hate rather than love, we lose G-d's special protection and are left to the mercy of the nations around us.[108]

---

108 Interestingly, the First Temple was destroyed because of the three cardinal sins of idol worship, immorality, and murder, while it took only one reason to warrant the destruction of the Second Temple (baseless hatred) — showing how bad hatred

I Didn't Know That!

The Golden Age of Spain was a time of comfort and ease for Spanish Jews. With the arrival of the Spanish Inquisition, life turned into a nightmare full of oppression, unbearable taxation, forced conversion, and torture. King Ferdinand and Queen Isabella of Spain ordered the expulsion in 1492, rejecting the arguments and pleas of their loyal Minister of Finance, Don Isaac Abarbanel, who was also the leader of the Jewish community and a great Torah sage. In his commentary to the book of Jeremiah, he wrote, "When the king decreed in the year 5252 (1492) that all Jews were to be expelled from his kingdom and were to leave within three months — the deadline being Tisha B'Av — the king had no idea of the date, yet he was guided from Heaven to set the deadline for that day."

Silver Lining of Tisha B'Av

The story is told of Napoleon walking through the streets of Paris. As he passed by a synagogue, he heard the sound of people weeping inside. He turned to his assistant and asked, "What's going on inside there?"

"The Jews are mourning the loss of their Temple."

"Who destroyed their Temple?" the emperor responded. "I didn't give anyone permission to do that!"

---

is. Also, the Talmud (*Yoma* 9a) says that the punishment for unwarranted hatred is so great that, while the first exile lasted only seventy years, we are still awaiting redemption from the second destruction, 2,000 years later.

"Today is the Ninth of Av and the Jews are crying over the loss of their Temple in Jerusalem, almost 2,000 years ago," was the reply.

Napoleon looked toward the synagogue and said, "If the Jews are still crying after so many years, then I am certain the Temple will one day be rebuilt!"

The silver lining of the Ninth of Av is that it reminds us what life is really about. By remembering our past, we contribute towards our future.

Preparation and Practices:

Shivah Asar B'Tammuz (and the Three Weeks), literally the Seventeenth of the month of Tammuz, is a minor fast-day commemorating the breaching of the walls of Jerusalem[109] by foreign conquerors and other tragedies[110] (e.g., the breaking of the tablets containing the Ten Commandments;[111]

---

109 This event led to the conquering of Jerusalem by our enemies and the destruction of the Temples soon after.

110 *Taanit* 4:6

111 Moses was at the top of Mount Sinai when he received the Ten Commandments. Upon descending the mountain to give them to the Jewish People, he saw them engaged in the sin of the Golden Calf — idolatry. He then smashed the tablets. This breaking is considered a great tragedy; the Jewish People were so unworthy and fickle in their service of G-d that the tablets themselves had to be broken.

the service in the First Temple was suspended;[112] a Torah scroll was burned by the wicked Greek Apostamus;[113] and an idol was set up in the Temple in Jerusalem.)[114] As we approach the Ninth of Av, we prepare ourselves by adopting, progressively, certain aspects of mourning. For example, Jewish weddings do not occur in the three weeks before the Ninth of Av and the nine days from the first of the month of Av until the fast itself have added restrictions[115] as

---

112 Prior to destruction of the First Temple, the regular daily offering was suspended on this day because we ran out of offerings due to the siege of Jerusalem. [Rashi explains the reason was because the government at the time forbade it.] The offerings were our way of showing appreciation for all G-d does for us as well as atoning for our sins and being unable to bring them was a serious loss.

113 Apostamus was a Greek officer in the times of the Second Temple. His burning of a Torah scroll was not only a great religious offense and tragedy, but was also representative of the Greek desire to wipe out Judaism. Furthermore, the burning set a precedent for the oft-repeated burning of Jewish books throughout the centuries. Living in our modern age of computers, it is important for us to keep in mind that until the invention and development of the printing press, all manuscripts were painstakingly copied by hand, so the losses involved in book burning were very serious. Many manuscripts were lost forever, and many students lost their primary access to the Jewish tradition — its sources.

114 For the religion that brought pure monotheism to the world, you can't get much worse than this.

115 Such as not eating meat, drinking wine, or bathing for pleasure

well. The fast of the Seventeenth of Tammuz occurs in the summer and lasts from sunrise until sunset. The goal of this period is to motivate us to introspect and improve our behaviors and attitudes.

Seudah Hamafseket: During the afternoon before the fast of Tisha B'Av, we eat a full meal in order to help us make it through the next day. Closer to the fast, we eat[116] the *Seudah Hamafseket*.[117] It consists of symbols of mourning to help get us into the right mindset: bread, water, and a hard-boiled egg.[118] The egg is considered a symbol of mourning because its round shape reminds us of the cycle of life. An egg also hardens as it is cooked, symbolizing the Jewish People who have become stronger due to our travails. This "sad" meal is eaten alone on the floor.

Do-Nots: Many of the prohibitions of Tisha B'Av are similar to those of Yom Kippur. We do not eat or drink, bathe, or anoint ourselves with oils, wear leather shoes, or have intimate relations. The overall goal is different, though. On Yom Kippur, many of the same laws arise out of a desire to temporarily leave the physical world and be fully focused on spirituality. Today, these restrictions come from a place of sadness and restriction.

---

116 Finishing before sunset
117 Which literally means "the meal that breaks" between the regular day and the fast
118 Some also dip the egg in ashes

The Book of Lamentations is read publicly on Tisha B'Av in a moving and unique melody. In it, the prophet Jeremiah hauntingly describes the destruction of Jerusalem and the sins of the Jewish People that caused it.

Special Prayers and Limited Study: Synagogue lights are kept low and the Ark's curtain is removed. Prayers are chanted in a soft, mournful voice, out of anguish over the loss of our direct connection to G-d. Since learning Torah is a joyful activity, we refrain from doing so on this day, except for "sadder subjects" such as the laws of mourning and of Tisha B'Av. We chant medieval dirges called Kinot which describe many tragedies throughout the centuries.

Tisha B'Av Fast Facts

Name: Tisha B'Av literally means "the ninth day of [the month of] Av."

Summary: We fast, pray, and mourn the destruction of the Temple in Jerusalem, the ensuing loss of spirituality in the world, and many other tragedies that occurred on this day. Prohibitions include eating, drinking, bathing, anointing with oil, wearing leather shoes, intimate relations, and studying pleasurable parts of Torah. Special mourning poems, Kinot, are recited.

Timing: Ninth day of Av, in the summer, and lasts for one night and one day.

Questions for Discussion:[119]

1. What happened on the Ninth of Av? Name as many tragedies as you can.
2. What are the similarities and differences of Tisha B'Av and Yom Kippur?
3. Why was the Temple destroyed?
4. What are Kinot?
5. Why don't we study Torah on Tisha B'Av?
6. What can be done to increase love and unity among the Jewish People?

---

119 Many answers can be offered to these questions. Here are a few ideas to help your discussion. (1) See the list above. (2) Many of the same prohibitions exist but the goals and overall feeling are quite different. Yom Kippur is a beautiful and happy day on which we "leave physicality" to uplift ourselves and resemble the angels; on Tisha B'Av we restrict ourselves out of sadness and mourning. (3) The First Temple was destroyed because of idol worship, immorality, and bloodshed. The Temple was rebuilt after seventy years, indicating that these sins had, for the most part, disappeared. The Second Temple was destroyed because of baseless hatred. Since it has not yet been rebuilt, we still are afflicted by this problem. (4) Sad elegies, poems, describing various tragedies of the day, recited on Tisha B'Av. (5) Torah study brings pleasure. (6) All ideas welcome!

Chapter 10:
Rosh Chodesh

"May it be Your will, O G-d ... that the coming month be one of goodness and blessing; May You grant us a long life, of peace, goodness, blessing, sustenance, health, respect ... a life full of prosperity and honor, of love for the Torah ... Amen."[120]

The moon can appear at any time during September, October or any other of the Western months. This is because the Western, or Gregorian, calendar's months are solar; the moon cycle is basically irrelevant. In contrast, Jewish months are lunar and a new Jewish month always coincides with the new moon beginning to appear.

The new moon, and thus the new month, symbolizes the change of the seasons, new beginnings, and the cycle of our lives. The Torah itself attaches great importance[121] to Rosh Chodesh, the new moon. In Temple times, the High Court in Jerusalem would

---

120 From Shabbat prayers, on the Shabbat before Rosh Chodesh
121 Its offerings are similar to and listed beside those of the other holidays (see Numbers 28).

sanctify the new month, trumpets would announce its arrival, unique and beautiful songs would be sung, special services would occur in the Temple, and torches would be lit. Even today, the occurrence of the new month is a special and meaningful day. We dress up, eat fancier meals, and sing special prayers and songs.

Women's Holiday

Rosh Chodesh is considered to be a special holiday for women. Medieval commentator Rashi explains[122] that when some errant members of the Jewish People were beginning to build the Golden Calf, they asked their wives to donate their gold and jewelry to its construction. The women refused to contribute to idol worship. They were given the holiday of Rosh Chodesh as a reward for their loyalty and trust in G-d.

Why was Rosh Chodesh in particular chosen to be the reward? The twelve months represented and corresponded to the twelve tribes of Israel. Once the tribes sinned in the building of the Golden Calf, Rosh Chodesh — the new month — was transferred over to those who did not make the same mistake: the loyal and committed women of Israel.[123]

Furthermore, the moon's cycle is closely connected

---

122 on *Megillah* 22b
123 *Menoras Hamaor*

to a woman's natural cycle. The new month represents new life, new creation, and the cycle of nature, and it is thus appropriate that it is particularly celebrated by women.

Never Give Up

The Jewish People is compared to the moon because just like the moon seems to disappear but returns again and again, so too, the Jewish People never gives up and keeps coming back again and again. Despite countless attacks and attempts at our demise, our ancestors never gave up and succeeded in passing on their Jewish identity to the next generation. The new month reminds us to bounce back from our reversals and never give up.

The First Mitzvah

Surprisingly, the very first mitzvah given to the Jewish People was the mitzvah to sanctify the new month. Why? Shouldn't Shabbat have come first? Or belief in G-d? Or one of the more "central" aspects of Judaism?

In order to answer this question, we need to know something fundamental about the Jewish calendar: it is real. We don't simply commemorate Passover as the Time of Our Freedom, or Yom Kippur as the

Day of Atonement and forgiveness. Rather, actually embedded into these days are particular spiritual energies. By celebrating them in their proper times, we access these energies in ways that are impossible at other times of the year. Rosh Chodesh was thus given as the first mitzvah because it is the key to establishing a properly functioning calendar and all of our holy days and commemorations. In order for our entire calendar to "tap into" the holiness of the day, the first holiday given was the new month — because the other holidays depend on it!

Furthermore, the commandment concerning Rosh Chodesh is actually to establish when the new month took place and to then sanctify it. By having this commandment as the very first mitzvah we received, a profound lesson was taught: our actions are significant. In performing the commandments, we are not robots. We are choosing to affect our own lives and the world itself. We establish what life will be like and we sanctify ourselves and our communities. By having this commandment as the very first mitzvah we received, we learned that we are truly important.

Chapter 11:
Shabbat

More than Israel has kept the Sabbath, the Sabbath has kept Israel.[124]

(Ahad Ha-am)

Enjoyed in a relaxed and happy atmosphere, Shabbat is the most important holiday in the Jewish calendar. Shabbat is a day of eating, drinking, enjoying — and above all, a day of rest. Adam and Eve actually "rested" from their "work" on Shabbat when they lived in the Garden of Eden, which begs the question: since all their physical needs were provided for them and they didn't have to "work" at all, why did they need to "rest"?[125]

---

124 Christian missionaries have been sent throughout the world proclaiming their leader as the "Savior" of the Jews. Our Ethiopian brothers and sisters had a wonderful response when the missionaries started targeting their Jewish communities: "No, you misunderstand," they replied. "Shabbat is the savior of the Jews."

125 Furthermore, why did G-d, Himself, need to "rest" on the seventh day? Can G-d become tired? The answer to this question is that G-d didn't need to rest at all, but rather stopped creating on the seventh day, thus teaching us to do

The **answer** lies in the fact that Shabbat is a spiritual rest more than a physical one and the "work" we abstain from is not "work" as is commonly defined today. During the first six days, G-d "created" and transformed nature. On the seventh day, G-d stopped creating. We give testimony to G-d's creation of the universe by doing the same. Six days of the week we build, change, and improve the world. On the seventh, we cease trying to build the world, acknowledging that G-d created the universe and remains in control. On Shabbat we rest[126] like G-d rested.

Jewish law delineates many Shabbat rules, whose common denominator is to turn our focus away from building, working, and planning, and help us appreciate being, connecting, and enjoying. Note that the laws of Shabbat[127] are suspended in life and death

---

the same.

126 The Talmud (*Shabbat* 130a) tells the story of a dove that was created without wings. Wobbling around on the ground, all the other creatures could run quicker than it. It complained to G-d, who then gave it wings. The dove found that with the addition of the wings, its running was even slower and once again complained to G-d, who then explained that the wings will allow the little dove to fly quickly and high in the sky. Similarly, those who don't understand the purpose of the Shabbat laws may feel weighed down by them, when in essence they really can let us soar!

127 And almost all of the commandments, with limited but important exceptions such as murder, rape, and idol worship

situations,[128] for Judaism is meant to enhance and deepen our lives rather than put us in danger.

Many thinkers throughout the ages have considered the Sabbath one of the great Jewish contributions to the world. Renowned author and psychologist Erich Fromm marveled at Shabbat, calling it a "release from the chains of time." Indeed, Shabbat has often been called a "Sanctuary in Time"; we spend our lives conquering the world, acquiring, and building. Yet time cannot be conquered — it always outlasts us. On Shabbat, therefore, we sanctify time. We discover its holiness.

The laws and rituals of Shabbat help us learn to feel complete — all of our work is done. Shabbat is like taking a deep breath and letting all the tension out; a day of joy, friendship, happiness, trust, lack of worries or pressures, and beautiful connections to spirituality and meaning.

Peace in the Home

One of the main goals of celebrating Shabbat is to deepen and strengthen the relationships between

---

128 The source for this suspension is a verse in Leviticus (18:5), "*And you shall live by them,*" meaning not to die on account of the *mitzvot*. Even in a case where life may or may not be at stake (i.e., two doctors disagree), we suspend the laws and save the life.

a husband and wife, and with our children. The struggle to make a living can too often take a toll on our relationships. Dedicating one day a week to spending time together reminds us how important our relationships are the rest of the week as well.

Equality of Shabbat

Our modern world has been so influenced by Jewish ideas that it is hard for us to imagine the scope of the philosophical, moral, and religious revolution that Judaism created. Monotheism was the first and most prominent revolutionary concept we offered the world. Shabbat was a close second.

Today, weekends off and vacations are the norm in most parts of the world. Yet before our ancestors were given Shabbat, the wealthy never worked and the poor never stopped working. There was no day off. The master could force you to work any time he wanted. The masses of humanity were chattel, at their masters' beck and call with never a moment to rest. As we declare in the Shabbat prayers, on Shabbat even the "maidservant" and "manservant" must rest — the master had no right to make them work. Yet it wasn't just one day of freedom they were granted; the very fact that an external law limited the master's power established a powerful principle of equality: that the human master was really not "The Master." Shabbat reminds employees and employers that G-d is the true Master. It is no wonder that tyrants have always opposed Shabbat — it is a challenge to their authority. For on Shabbat, we are all equal. Whether rich or poor, powerful or powerless, on Shabbat we all are equal. On Shabbat, we are all royalty.

Dale Carnegie's Shabbat Experiment

Dale Carnegie once talked about an experiment where the overall productivity of two types of workers was measured. The first group worked straight without breaks carrying heavy iron castings. The second group did the same work, but would spend *the majority* of its time resting between loads. Guess who was more productive …

The second group. Although it may have looked like the first group was doing more — since they were always moving — in reality, the second group accomplished more.

It is a fascinating experiment, but the results are not so surprising nowadays. The modern world recognizes that a person needs to rest in order to be more productive. Vacations, coffee breaks, and weekends are all an accepted part of business productivity.

Interestingly, the lessons of this experiment were not always accepted, and the Romans — including their greats such as Seneca and Juvenal — thought the Jews lazy for our abstention from work on the seventh day. Egyptian-Jewish philosopher Philo responded that frequent breaks let us return to our work with renewed vigor. Philo was certainly correct. At a deeper level, though, he was answering the Romans at their level of understanding — that regular periods of rest help overall productivity.

In its essence, though, Shabbat is neither a twenty-four-hour coffee break nor an accessory to the rest of the week. Shabbat is the goal we aim for, the center of our lives. Shabbat is actually the pinnacle of the week, not just a rest in order to help the other six days.[129] It is such an important aspect of Jewish life that it is the only "ritual" observance in the Ten Commandments, and is mentioned in the Torah more often than any other commandment. We look forward to it. Delicious food is set aside for it and our finest clothes are worn

---

129 Evidence of this is in the names of the days of the week in Hebrew. There is no word for "Sunday" or "Monday" in Hebrew. The weekdays are referred only in their relationship to Shabbat: "the first day to Shabbat," "the second day to Shabbat," etc. We are constantly reminded of the centrality of Shabbat because it is the only day that actually has a name of its own.

on it. Shabbat is the center[130] of the week and at the center of our minds and hearts.

Shabbat represents everything that life should be; it is full of spirituality, family, meaning, happiness, and love. During the rest of the week, we are involved in creating, building, achieving, and changing the world. It is appropriate and important for us to make a living and try and improve the world. Shabbat reminds us of the essence of life — relationships with our family, friends and G-d. We do not rest on Shabbat in order to have a more productive week. Rather, we work during the week in order to be able to truly appreciate the celebration of Shabbat.

> ### I Didn't Know That!
> Rabbi Noah Weinberg suggested an innovative way to get into the Shabbat mood. Next Friday, when the sun is going down, clench your fists tight for sixty seconds and then let go. "That, my friends," he concludes, "is Shabbat."

Preparation and Practices

Preparing for Shabbat: Erev Shabbat (the day before Shabbat) includes preparation such as cleaning, cooking, taking a warm bath or shower, and getting

---

130 Like the center of a cube with six sides

dressed in our finest clothing. Aside from the practical aspects of these activities, Shabbat preparation also helps bring on the Shabbat atmosphere. When we[131] get involved in preparing for Shabbat, we gain from the day itself.

Tzedakah: There is a custom to give *tzedakah* (charity) just before lighting Shabbat candles as a way of "giving something" before we receive the gift of Shabbat. Many people have a little *pushkah* (charity tin) by their candles for this purpose.

Candlelighting: G-d began the creation of the world with light,[132] and thus we begin our celebration of creation with the lighting of candles.[133] On a practical level, before electricity, candlelight allowed people to see their food and thus enjoy it more, and prevented household mishaps, thus adding to peace in the home. But there are deeper levels. The burning flames of the

---

131 In fact, the Talmud (*Shabbat* 119a) recounts that even wealthy ancient sages who had enough servants to take care of all the preparation would still do different things to get ready for Shabbat.

132 "Let there be light!"

133 As Lori Palatnik writes in *Friday Night and Beyond*, "It is the woman who brings light into the home ... the tone, the feel, the look ... it is from her. When she is happy and positive, even the most depressed husband or tired child will absorb her energy and be lifted."

Shabbat candles[134] captivate us. Their dancing on the wicks[135] draws us in. Their light illuminates the dark. The candles provide a sense of warmth, joy, and peace that typify the sublime spirit of the Sabbath.

Kabbalat Shabbat: A beautiful short prayer service called "Kabbalat Shabbat" (welcoming the Shabbat) was created by rabbis living in northern Israel about 400 years ago.[136] There, the sages would dress in white and enter the orchards, singing to welcome the Shabbat bride. The most famous song is the beautiful "Lecha Dodi,"[137] whose verses reflect this bride metaphor.

----

134 Traditionally, two candles are lit. Many explanations exist for this. One candle is for "*Zachor*," the positive remembrance of Shabbat, and one is for "*Shamor*," the prohibitions of Shabbat. Alternatively, one is for the woman, and one for her husband. This explanation fits particularly well with the custom of adding a new candle for each new child in the family — they each add light to the world.

135 As Rabbi Jonathan Bressel explains in the *Shabbat Table Guide*, just as a non-physical flame rests on a physical wick, so too does our non-physical soul rest on our physical bodies. We are thus reminded that Shabbat is a day of spirituality — a day of the soul.

136 Although the Talmud mentions various special ways the sages would welcome Shabbat, and the words said were mostly written by King David, the actual prayer service was composed much later.

137 Written by Rabbi Shlomo Alkabetz of sixteenth-century Israel.

Shalom Aleichem: Literally these words mean "peace be upon you." This beautiful short song is chanted upon our return from shul on Friday night before the meal begins. Tradition says two angels accompany us home, a good angel and a bad angel. If upon their arrival the house is ready for Shabbat, the good one says, "May it be so next week" and the bad one is forced to agree. If not, the reverse happens. In this song we welcome the angels, ask for their blessing, and wish them well on their departure.

Eishet Chayil: Traditionally sung at the beginning of Shabbat, this song is usually sung by the husband in appreciation of the woman of the home. The "Woman of Valor" (as the title is usually translated) is a husband's trusted friend and partner, full of loving kindness, helps to provide for the home, gives thoughtful advice, and is a role model to those around her. The verses particularly emphasize her trust in G-d.[138]

Blessings of Children: At the beginning of Shabbat, we give each[139] of our children a beautiful

---

138 Taken from the Book of Proverbs (31:10–31), these verses are understood to have been composed by King Solomon, although some explain that Abraham himself wrote them. Since Shabbat is the bride of the Jewish People, it is fitting that we sing a love song to our brides at this time.

139 The blessing for daughters includes the prayer that they

blessing. The words traditionally said during this tender moment refer to physical health and well being, spiritual growth, a sense of inner peace and positive relationships.

Kiddush: We usher in Shabbat by making a blessing[140] over a full cup of kosher wine or grape juice. Blessings do not make the wine "holy," rather we use the wine to bless G-d and to add to the holiness of Shabbat. Many people use a nice silver goblet to add honor to this beautiful day.

Washing Hands: Before eating bread, we ritually wash our hands and say a blessing. This washing is not for hygienic purposes, but rather a reminder that our eating is more than just a physical act. By slowing us down, this hand-washing teaches us that we are not animals jumping at whatever food is thrown in front of us; we are elevated enough to pause and add

---

should grow up like the Matriarchs, for they epitomize the good qualities we are to aspire to. Interestingly enough, the blessing for sons refers to Ephraim and Menashe, Joseph's two sons, and not the Patriarchs. Growing up in a decadent Egyptian culture and yet remaining strong loyal Jews, they are role models for those growing up in the Diaspora. Furthermore, they were the first Jewish siblings to live without rivalry (there was no strife when their blessings were switched; check Genesis 48 for details).

140 The verses said on Friday night recall both the creation of the world and our departure from Egypt; a different text is used on the Shabbat morning *Kiddush*.

meaning to our actions.

Shabbat Food: Central to the celebration of Shabbat are the Shabbat meals. Shabbat meals bring together family and friends for delicious food, delightful conversation, singing, and inspiration. On Shabbat, we are not rushed — we enjoy life and each other. On Shabbat, we eat the best food of the week. While many Western Jews are used to traditional Eastern European food, in reality Shabbat meals can include almost any type of cuisine. The important thing is that the food is tasty and plentiful.

Wine and Challah: Shabbat is famous for the wine or grape juice that is used for the blessings and enjoyed during the meals. Nowadays, delicious kosher wines are available from the USA, Israel, Europe, Chile, Argentina, Australia, and elsewhere. One of the most beloved aspects of the Shabbat meal is the sweet challah[141] (bread) that is served[142] with each meal. We

---

141 Aside from its delicious taste, there is great symbolism to the centrality of challah to the Shabbat meal. What is significant about the bread? Bread represents our staple diet, and traditionally it is the basic definition of a meal rather than a snack. Going through eleven stages of human production, by using bread we show that humanity has a share in the development of the world. By making a blessing, we emphasize that in reality, everything we do depends on G-d.

142 The bread is dipped in salt like the offerings in the ancient Temple in Jerusalem, reminding us that our table should be

use two *challot* at each of the Shabbat meals, reminding us of the special Manna-food that sustained the Jewish People in the desert: it fell in double portions (thus our two *challot*) on Friday to avoid us having to gather it on Shabbat. Like the Manna, the challah is covered and many have a special cloth for this purpose. The Shabbat challah is traditionally braided. Braids are shapes not found anywhere in nature, thus symbolizing that Shabbat is a meta-physical experience, reaching past the material world and touching our souls.

Fish and Cholent: Jews traditionally eat fish during Shabbat, most famously "Gefilte Fish."[143] What is the connection between fish and Shabbat?[144] In

---

as holy as an altar. Furthermore, salt is "eternal," so to speak, like the Jewish People, and can either hurt or heal (e.g., salt on a wound or healing salts), thus reminding us to use our talents for good purposes rather than selfish ones.

143 How do you know which fish in the pond is *gefilte* fish? Answer: It is the one with the slice of carrot on top.

144 The connection has been explained even further, though. In the Torah's account of Noah's Flood, the only living beings to survive outside the ark were ... fish! Since they had not been corrupted as all other creatures had, they made it through the ordeal unscathed. Their elevated nature is also attested to by the fact that they require no ritual slaughter like other living animals we are allowed to eat. This special status makes them fitting for Shabbat (*Or Hashabbat*). One more note: fish eyes are always open, signifying that G-d is always watching us and protecting us. On Shabbat, we remind ourselves of this fact.

Hebrew, fish is called *dag*, made up of the two letters *dalet* and *gimel*, which are respectively the fourth and third letters of the Hebrew alphabet. The word's numerical value is thus seven, corresponding to the seventh day.[145]

For the Shabbat Day meal, many also eat a warm, slow-cooked[146] stew. The European version is called *cholent*, possibly from the French words *chaud* and *lent*, meaning hot and slow, respectively. It is called *schena* in Morocco, *tbit* in Yemen, *hetteh* in Kurdestan, and *hmin* in Yemen. Whichever version you eat, this delicious dish is much loved.

Third Meal: In olden times, people used to eat one main meal a day. The Shabbat evening meal was the central meal of Friday and the Shabbat morning lunch was the central meal of Saturday. By adding an extra meal (called *Seudah Shlishit* or *Shalosh Seudos*) at the end of Shabbat afternoon, we emphasize the goodness and abundance of Shabbat — and life.

Havdalah: Just as Shabbat started with lighting candles, smelling challah, and making a blessing over wine, so too we formally end Shabbat with a beautiful ceremony including lighting a flame, a blessing over

---

145 Incredibly, wine's Hebrew name, *yayin*, adds up to seventy, and challah equals forty-three, both of whose "fundamental" number is seven.

146 In accordance with the rules of Shabbat

wine, and smelling spices. The ceremony is called *Havdalah*, which literally means separation, and the text we recite emphasizes our ability to distinguish between the holy and the profane. We wish each other a *"Shavua Tov"* (*Gutte voch* in Yiddish), which means "a good week."

Melaveh Malkah: A host always wants an important guest to stay a little longer, and so we too try to keep the Shabbat feeling a little longer by having a small meal in its honor. The words *melaveh malkah* literally mean, "escorting the queen," as we are at this point escorting the Shabbat Queen as she leaves us until next week.

Shabbat Fast Facts

Name: Shabbat literally means "rest" or "cease", for on it G-d stopped creating the world.

Summary: The seventh day of every week is a day of celebration. We spend time with friends and family, eat wonderful meals, sing, read, join the community in prayer, and get inspired.

Timing: Every week of the year, from before sunset on Friday until Saturday night.

Questions for Discussion:[147]

1. Explain what the word Shabbat means.
2. Read Ahad Ha-am's quotation at the beginning of this chapter. How do you understand it?
3. Is Shabbat a means to an end or the goal itself?
4. How does Shabbat help family life?
5. How does Shabbat help the Jewish People?
6. How has Shabbat affected the world?

---

147 Most of these questions have numerous answers. Here are a few ideas for easy reference, to help your discussion: (1) It means to stop or cease, as G-d stopped creating on this day, as we do as well. (2) Shabbat has regularly kept the Jewish People focused on their identity. (3) Both. It helps us be more effective and focused and relaxed during the week, but also represents the "other worldly" dimension of life that we strive for. (4) It brings the family together for quality time once a week. (5) See #2 above. Also, it reminds us of our uniqueness and builds communal ties through synagogue and celebration. (6) Shabbat taught the world that rest is an important part of life.

Conclusion

Rabbi Samson Raphael Hirsch once commented that, "A Jew's calendar is his catechism." Nowadays, not really knowing what catechism is, the point is often lost. Still, the remark became quite famous in its time because it encapsulated a central idea to Jewish thought.

For a Catholic, the catechism is the oft-repeated encapsulation of belief. Rabbi Hirsch was explaining that Jews don't need to summarize and state our belief system with any regularity. Of course, Judaism does indeed have beliefs that are central to its system — Maimonides enumerated thirteen of them. However, Jewish life itself expresses our beliefs. The redemption from Egypt is not simply a historical fact; it is an emotional and philosophical experience that we relive at Passover. On Rosh Hashanah we recognize that G-d is truly the Ultimate Authority, the King of kings. Yom Kippur offers us forgiveness and purity of heart. Each holiday is a floor in the building of Jewish belief, experience, and identity. On a weekly basis, celebrating Shabbat encapsulates Jewish belief and life like no other experience. Each Friday night we "stop" building and creating things to remind ourselves that G-d stopped and commanded us to do so as well. To appreciate what we have. To connect with our families, the Jewish community, and G-d. To become a little deeper.

Of course there is more to Judaism than the holidays. There are many commandments and traditions (being kind, keeping kosher, and honesty, to name a few) that have little if anything to do with the holidays at all and they are vital, central to our beliefs and way of life. But for many of us, it is the holidays that really stand out in our Jewish memories. Our intellectual and emotional lives are intertwined with the Jewish calendar. And our beliefs are strengthened from it. It is the holidays that remind us that we're Jewish.

In a sense, the holidays *make* us Jewish.

Enjoy them!

Recommended Reading on the Jewish Holidays

The Book of Our Heritage by Rabbi Eliyahu Kitov: a classic in-depth look at the relevant laws and traditions of each holiday.

Friday Night and Beyond (Jason Aronson, Inc.) by Lori Palatnik: a user-friendly, practical guide to Shabbat.

Halachos of _____ (Feldheim) by Rabbi Shimon Eider: each holiday has its own volume with detailed explanations of the laws and customs of the holiday.

The One-Hour Purim Primer (Leviathan Press) by Shimon Apisdorf: an interesting, concise, and informative description of Purim.

Rosh Hashanah and Yom Kippur Survival Kit (Leviathan Press) by Shimon Apisdorf: an inspirational and humorous paperback that helps transform the holidays into meaningful experiences.

Sabbath: Day of Eternity (National Conference of Synagogue Youth) by Rabbi Aryeh Kaplan; an inspirational and informative short explanation of why we do what we do on Shabbat, including a short guide to major laws.

The Sabbath (Feldheim) by Dayan Dr. Isidor Grunfield; a classic explanation of the concept of *melachah* (work) on Shabbat, and much of the philosophy of the day.

Seasons of the Soul (Mesorah Publications) by Rabbi Nisson Wolpin, editor; articles on the symbolism and meaning of the holidays.

The Survival Kit Family Haggadah (Leviathan Press) by Shimon Apisdorf; a popular, user-friendly Haggadah with humor, meaning, and clear explanations.

The First Ten Days (Feldheim) by Rabbi Yaacov Haber; a beautiful, uplifting guide to the first ten days of the year.

Sefiros by Rabbi Yaacov Haber (TorahLab) inspiration throughout the counting of the Omer.

About the Author

Doron Kornbluth is the author of the best-selling *Raising Kids to Love Being Jewish*, *Why Marry Jewish*, *Why Be Jewish*, and *Cremation or Burial? A Jewish View*. His essays have appeared all over the internet and his books have been translated into several other languages. A renowned international speaker, Doron is hosted in over fifty cities a year. He is also an inspirational (and licensed) tour guide in Israel. Doron is happily married and actively involved in raising his own Jewish family. His website is www.doronkornbluth.com.

About Mosaica Press

Mosaica Press is an independent publisher of Jewish books. Our authors include some of the most profound, interesting, and entertaining thinkers and writers in the Jewish community today. There is a great demand for high-quality Jewish works dealing with issues of the day — and **Mosaica Press** is helping fill that need. Our books are available around the world. Please visit us at www.mosaicapress.com.